BOBBY FLAY'S
GRILL IT!

BOBBY FLAY'S

GRILL IT!

Bobby Flay

with Stephanie Banyas and Sally Jackson

Photographs by Ben Fink

For my wife, Stephanie, whose enduring love and dedication are eclipsed only by her ferocious appetite.

Copyright © 2008 by Boy Meets Grill, Inc.
Photographs copyright © 2008 by Ben Fink

Published in the United States by Clarkson Potter/Publishers,
an imprint of the Crown Publishing Group, a division of Random
House, Inc., New York.
www.crownpublishing.com
www.clarksonpotter.com

Clarkson N. Potter is a trademark and Potter and colophon are
registered trademarks of Random House, Inc.

Library of Congress Cataloging-in-Publication Data
Flay, Bobby.
  [Grill it!]
  Bobby Flay's grill it! / Bobby Flay, with Stephanie
Banyas, and Sally Jackson. — 1st ed.
      p.   cm.
Includes index.
1. Barbecue cookery.   I. Banyas, Stephanie.
II. Jackson, Sally, 1978-   III. Title.   IV. Title: Grill it!
TX840.B3F56 2008
641.5'784—dc22   2007032662

ISBN 978-0-307-35142-5

Printed in Japan

Design by Wayne Wolf/Blue Cup Design

10 9 8 7 6 5 4 3 2 1

First Edition

Also by Bobby Flay

Bobby Flay's Mesa Grill Cookbook

Bobby Flay's Grilling for Life

Bobby Flay's Boy Meets Grill

Bobby Flay Cooks American

Bobby Flay's Boy Gets Grill

Bobby Flay's From My Kitchen to Your Table

Bobby Flay's Bold American Food

acknowledgments

Stephanie Banyas, Sally Jackson, Renee Forsberg, J.C. Pavlovich,
Andrea Toto, Ben Fink, Barb Fritz, Marysarah Quinn, Selina Cicogna,
Amy Boorstein, Joan Denman, Viking, Weber, Laurence Kretchmer,
Jerry Kretchmer, Jeff Bliss, Stephanie March, Dorothy Flay, and Bill Flay,
the staffs of Mesa Grill New York, Mesa Grill Las Vegas, Mesa Grill
Bahamas, Bolo, Bar Americain, and Bobby Flay Steak Atlantic City;
Food Network;
And to my editor, Rica Allannic . . . Thanks for all your hard work

contents

introduction

I have always loved eating almost anything hot off the grill. When I was a kid, I remember there would be smoke billowing out of the backyard as my dad took orders like a polished short-order cook in the busiest diner. "Do you want yours plain or with cheese?" he would ask. There were no other options—you were getting a hamburger or a cheeseburger and it was going to be well done. Period.

Firing up the grill makes every-night dinners with family or simple get-togethers with friends feel like a party or some sort of celebration. Everyone wants to take part in the action, and why not? It's probably going to involve lots of good tasting, healthy food and a frosty cocktail of some sort, which can only lead to lots of smiles. And as the clean-up is a lot easier than a dinner that involves breaking out every pot and pan in the closet, those happy faces remain long after the eating is done.

Grilling has come a long way since the overcooked burgers of my youth. It's widely regarded as a healthier alternative to frying in lots of butter or oil and the sweet smoky kiss of hardwood lump charcoal beats the taste of briquettes doused in lighter fluid any day. Today most grill cooks have widened their repertoires from hamburgers and hot dogs to a spectrum of simple but spectacular dishes. Next to the chopped meat there is now a place for fish and shellfish, pork and chicken, and, more popular than ever, a garden full of vegetables.

Not only have our grilling options expanded in terms of what we grill, but how we grill has changed, too. First there were only charcoal grills, then gas, and now, you can easily find one of the great grill pans out there so that you can bring the party inside and onto the stovetop. What was once only for summer you can now accomplish regardless of the season. (And, in fact, all of the recipes in this book can be cooked on a grill pan instead of outside.)

When I was thinking about *Grill It!,* I thought a lot about how my friends and I go about putting a meal together on the grill. It all starts with the shopping; often enough the planning of the menu doesn't start until I arrive at the farmer's market or grocery store. I want to be inspired by the ingredients before committing to a recipe. I want to walk up to the beautiful tomatoes or sweet corn, the pork chops or rib-eye steaks, and I want to see what looks best, what grabs my eye, what I'm craving.

This is the book to turn to when you know *what* you want but you don't know *how* you want it. Let's say you've passed a roadside stand with fresh corn and you couldn't resist picking up half a dozen ears. Maybe there was a special on salmon at your fish market—perfect, you've got dinner. Except what are you going to do with that corn and salmon now that you're home? That's where *Grill It!* comes in.

Turn to the corn chapter, see what's in your pantry, and take it from there. With nine recipes for corn—from steamed in the husk to grilled with flavored butters or taken off the cob and paired with other veggies to make a succotash—you're bound to find just the right way to take advantage of your roadside find. The same goes for that salmon—be it glazed, spice rubbed, or topped with a flavorful relish. *Grill It!* gives you all the options you need to turn your supermarket bounty into an awesome meal from the grill, chapter by simple chapter.

Because no one thinks, "I want to grill a main course and a side dish tonight"—we all think, "I want to do chicken breasts and maybe some summer squash"—the book's chapters are divided by ingredient. There is a chapter on asparagus, on scallops, one on just pork. . . . If burgers are what you are craving, then open up the chapter entitled simply "Burgers." You'll find not just beef burgers in there, but turkey and buffalo versions, too.

This is the book for the way we grill today with 150 simple recipes to turn to night after night. So go ahead—expand your repertoire beyond hamburgers and cheeseburgers. Now that you've got it, grill it! Just don't forget to light the grill first.

Bobby Flay

the grill

If I had a dime for every time someone asked me, "Bobby, what's the best grill?" or "Bobby, which is better, gas or charcoal?" I would be a very wealthy man. I am on record many times as saying that I prefer the ease and consistency of gas grills. However, that doesn't mean that I don't use charcoal grills myself from time to time. Charcoal burns hotter than gas, allowing for a better sear and more flavor from the smoke; but I have never had a problem getting a really good sear on the gas grill and I also like to add flavor to my food while it's grilling (with spice rubs and glazes) and after it comes off the heat (with vinaigrettes or salsas)—so for me, it's a wash.

I guess what I am trying to say is there is no right or wrong answer. A skilled griller could cook a gourmet meal with little more than a few logs of wood and a pack of matches. It's all about what works best for you. However, I can give you a few guidelines on what to look for when buying a grill to make the process a little bit easier.

Gas Grills

Price and Construction

Normally, like most things, the higher the price of the grill, the better the grill. That's not to say that there aren't some really good-quality grills that won't require you to remortgage the house. Set a price range that you can afford and then go out and find the best grill that you can in that range. Start by choosing one that is made from high-grade stainless steel. Next, give it a shake. Is it well built and sturdy or does it wobble and look like a strong wind could blow it over? The biggest differences between the less expensive brands and those that cost more are in construction and heat distribution. Both are important. A weak construction could be dangerous. If a gas grill isn't solid on the sales floor, chances are it will fall apart rather quickly on the patio or deck.

Heat distribution is key. Better gas grills generally have two or more separate burners (not just control knobs) which allow greater control of heat. Most lower-priced grills have only one burner shaped like an H or a bar, some with one control, some with two controls. Gas grills with one burner don't allow you to control heat as well as gas grills with multiple burners and may result in hot and cold spots on the cooking surface.

BTU's

BTU's are not a measure of cooking power. They indicate the volume of gas a grill can burn. In general, large grills with large cooking surfaces require higher BTU's. That said, well-engineered grills use fewer BTU's and cook food more efficiently, similar to a well-engineered car. Too many BTU's can cause damage to burners and reduce the life of the grill. A general rule to follow is to look for 100 BTU's per square inch of primary cooking space.

Charcoal Grills

Die-hard grillers prefer charcoal over gas. They tell me that there is nothing like the red-hot coals, flames, and smoke. I respect that and use charcoal myself when the mood strikes me. Charcoal grills are much less expensive than gas grills but the same criteria apply when purchasing one.

Price and Construction

Charcoal grills normally range in price from one hundred to five hundred dollars. Once again, a good solid construction is just as important for charcoal grills at it is for gas grills, maybe even more so since you are dealing with open fire and hot coals. You really don't need to go for any bells and whistles when looking for a charcoal grill but there are a few features that are nice to have and will make your life a little easier. Here is what I recommend:

- A porcelain-enamel finish on the bowl and lid make for a practically indestructible grill.
- A tight-fitting lid is necessary for cooking larger cuts of meat, which require indirect grilling.
- Top and bottom vents allow for good airflow to keep the coals going.
- Look for two grates—one in the bottom portion of the grill to lift coals and the other higher for cooking the food. The bottom grate allows the air to flow so that the charcoal burns and so that heat and smoke are circulated during cooking. Generally the grates sit on metal pieces welded to the body of the grill. Check the metal guides and make sure they are solidly attached.
- Hinged grill grates let you add additional charcoal easily while grilling.

- A model that includes a damper will allow you to sweep ashes into it so you aren't left having to scoop them out yourself.

Lump (Hardwood) Charcoal versus Charcoal Briquettes

I prefer lump charcoal over briquettes but I do use both for different reasons and different recipes, and sometimes I combine them. Lump charcoal gives a great woodsy aroma to food and briquettes provide long, even heat. Both burn equally hot but lump charcoal burns very hot and very quickly, which works well for quick-cooking items such as burgers, fish, and chicken breasts. If you want to grill long-cooking items such as a pork shoulder or brisket, then the slow, steady heat of the briquettes is the way to go.

Building a Fire

Don't even think about reaching for that can of lighter fluid. One of the single greatest inventions ever created for grilling is a chimney starter. This aluminum cylinder requires only charcoal, newspaper, and a match or lighter to create clean-burning, glowing bright red coals in less than 15 minutes. To use a chimney starter, follow these easy steps:

1. Stuff a few pieces of newspaper into the bottom of the chimney starter.
2. Remove the top grate of the grill. Place the chimney starter on the bottom grate of the grill, right side up.
3. Fill the top part of the chimney starter to the top with charcoal. Light the newspaper with a lighter or matches.
4. Heat the coals until they glow bright orange and turn ashy.
5. Carefully empty the coals evenly over the bottom of the grill.

You will get approximately an hour of grilling time from a large canister of coals so if you are planning on grilling something that takes longer to cook than an hour (such as brisket or pork butt), be sure to have another canister of hot coals ready to go to replenish the heat before it dips too low.

Direct versus Indirect

Confusing? It really is quite simple. Direct grilling literally means to grill the food right over the heat source and is used when grilling small, lean items that require minutes to cook, such as burgers, chicken breasts, fish, steaks, and vegetables.

Indirect grilling means to place the food to the side of the heat source instead of directly over the flame. This can be achieved by only igniting some burners on a gas grill or by piling coals to one side of a charcoal grill. A drip tray is placed below the food to prevent fat from the food from igniting and generating a flare-up. The indirect technique is normally used for larger, tougher cuts of meat that take at least an hour to cook, such as ribs, brisket, and whole turkeys, which would incinerate before cooking through if placed directly over the heat source.

How Hot?

Most gas grills come with a built-in thermometer that indicates exact Fahrenheit degrees or indicates Hot, Medium-Hot, Medium, and so forth. For gas grills without a thermometer or for charcoal grills, here's an easy way to gauge the heat by simply using your hand: Hold the palm of your hand flat about five inches above the coals and

count in seconds. If you can keep your hand over the coals:

1 to 2 seconds—the coals are hot
3 to 4 seconds—the coals are medium-hot
5 to 6 seconds—the coals are medium
6 to 7 seconds—the coals are medium-low
8 to 9 seconds—the coals are low

Controlling the Heat

If your fire is burning too hot, reduce the heat by spreading out the coals. If your fire is burning too low, increase the heat by pushing the coals closer together and adding more charcoal to the outer edges of the fire.

Testing for Doneness

The hardest thing about grilling food is knowing just when enough is enough. As a professional chef, I prefer the touch test, which is really easy and makes total sense. As meat cooks, it becomes firmer and firmer to the touch. Rare meat feels spongy, medium meat feels springy, and well-done feels taut. This is true for pork, poultry, and steak-like fish such as tuna, salmon, and swordfish, too.

If you use this method each time you grill, you will quickly learn to tell what a perfectly cooked piece of meat or fish feels like. However, if you have tried this method and it still doesn't work for you, my second suggestion would be to purchase an instant-read thermometer at your local grocery store or kitchen supply store. I even use these myself from time to time, especially when I am grilling a larger cut of meat or a whole chicken or turkey. Simply insert the thermometer into the center of the meat or fish to get the internal temperature reading. Remember to remove meat and chicken from the grill a few degrees below the desired doneness and to let it rest for at least 5 minutes before serving. Resting will allow the internal temperature to rise and the juices to recirculate. Also, it's better to undercook than overcook. You can always put food back on the grill if it's undercooked but there is little you can do to an overcooked piece of meat, chicken, or fish to make it moist again.

Gear

No one should be intimidated by grilling. Just think of your grill as an outdoor oven and you will be good to go. Once you decide on what type of grill you want (gas or charcoal), you will need a few other items that will have you looking and grilling like a pro in no time.

Chimney starter—The most important piece of equipment ever invented for the charcoal grill. If you are using charcoal, there is no excuse not to have one of these. Throw out that can of lighter fluid now!

Heavy-duty grill brush—It's really important to keep the cooking surface of your grill clean. Baked-on food can completely ruin the taste of your dish. It's easiest to do with one of these

brushes. Scrub the grates while the grill is still warm.

Brushes—These are crucial for applying glazes, sauces, and oils. The pastry brushes that you find in home stores can be pricey, so pay a visit to your local hardware store and pick up a few paint brushes, which are less expensive and work equally as well.

Tongs—I can't grill vegetables, shellfish, or steaks without tongs. Don't bother with those long-handled grilling tongs normally found in the barbecue section of your home store. Get intimate with your grill and opt for the regular stainless-steel tongs from the housewares section of most large, general retailers.

Fish spatula/heavy-duty metal spatula—These spatulas are wider and have a longer metal base than regular spatulas, which makes them perfect for sliding underneath food so that you can carefully turn whole fish and burgers without having them fall apart.

Meat thermometer—An instant-read thermometer is your best bet for making sure that meat and fish are cooked to the proper temperature.

Squeeze bottles—These inexpensive plastic bottles are perfect for storing sauces, oils, and vinaigrettes. They also allow you to control the amount of dressing you put on salads and other dishes. You can pick these up at restaurant supply stores as well as kitchen and housewares stores.

White terrycloth towels—I prefer to use these towels (also known as bar towels) instead of bulky potholders. They are perfect for cleaning off the edges of serving plates and tackling spills as well.

the pantry

The recipes in this book are inspired by a lot of different cuisines, but that doesn't mean you need to stock your pantry with a hundred different items. In my opinion, if you cook frequently, the following list of ingredients should always be in your pantry. Not only will you be able to prepare any of the recipes in this book, but you can also experiment with the staples on your own and create new recipes. Remember that the refrigerator should be viewed as your pantry, too. I like to refer to it as a cold pantry, where things like fresh herbs, citrus, and ginger should always be on hand to add flavor to any recipe.

Dry Storage

Anchovies—I recommend anchovies packed in olive oil in glass jars, not cans.

Beans—Dried beans are my preference at my restaurants, but the ease of canned beans can't be ignored at home and I definitely recommend them when time isn't on your side.

Dried chiles and chile powder—It's no secret that dried chiles play an important role in my cooking. They are available in almost every market today and online.

Garlic—Look for solid, firm heads. Don't buy it if it feels light or hollow; it's old.

Jams and preserves—I love creating glazes for meat and fish from jams and preserves. I particularly like apricot, orange, and plum.

Oils—I use a variety of oils in my cooking: canola oil (or a canola–olive oil blend), olive oil, extra-virgin olive oil, and sesame oil. I use canola for just about everything because of its neutral flavor and tolerance for high heat. I brush meat and vegetables with it just before putting them on the grill, add it to marinades, and use it the majority of the time in my full-flavored vinaigrettes. I turn to regular, or "pure," olive oil when cooking a Mediterranean-inspired recipe over high heat. Extra-virgin olive oil is best saved for finishing off a dish and for making simple vinaigrettes where its fruity flavor won't get overwhelmed by other ingredients. Sesame oil is another fantastic flavor enhancer for finished dishes and marinades. Make sure to get the dark, toasted sesame variety; it has much more flavor than light sesame oil.

Onions—I always have red and Spanish onions in my pantry because most of my recipes include one or the other. I also love sweet onions such as Vidalia for just grilling and eating.

Potatoes and sweet potatoes—I always have sweet potatoes and a few varieties of white-, yellow-, and red-skinned potatoes.

Shallots—The flavor of a shallot is a cross between that of onion and garlic. I love using shallots in sauces and vinaigrettes.

Soy sauce—I use a lot of kosher salt in my cooking, which has a milder flavor than iodized salt, so when I create a recipe that calls for soy sauce, I prefer using the low-sodium variety over the regular variety for the same reason.

Spices—I like to buy my spices whole and grind them in a coffee/spice grinder. Not only do they taste better when you do this, but whole spices will last longer in your pantry, too.

Sweeteners—I use brown sugar, honey, maple syrup, and molasses not only for sweetness but to also balance flavors in my cooking.

Vinegar—I love vinegar and always have at least five varieties in my pantry at all times. If you don't have the room, make sure to have at least red or white wine vinegar, balsamic or aged sherry vinegar, and rice vinegar.

Cold Storage

Butter—I prefer using unsalted butter because it allows me to control the amount of salt in my cooking and the flavor is fresher than that of salted butter.

Capers—Capers are the flower bud of a bush native to the Mediterranean and parts of Asia. After the buds are harvested, they are dried in the sun and then pickled in vinegar, brine, wine, or salt. I prefer the variety pickled in vinegar.

Citrus—I love the fresh flavor that citrus juice gives to a marinade or vinaigrette, and I always have fresh lemons, limes, and oranges on hand. Don't forget to use the zest; it's more flavorful than the juice.

Cornichons—These tiny sour French pickles add great flavor to salads and tartar sauces.

Dairy products—My go-to ingredients are crème fraîche, sour cream, Greek yogurt, buttermilk, and all sorts of cheeses.

Ginger—Fresh ginger actually lasts a long time when properly stored in an airtight bag. In fact, you can even break off pieces of it, wrap them, and store in the freezer for months.

Herbs—With proper care, fresh herbs will last in your refrigerator for at least 3 days. When you bring them home from the grocery store, do not wash them. Wrap them in dry paper towels and store them in a plastic zip-top bag in the refrigerator. Placing them in the refrigerator wet or even slightly damp will cause them to go bad quickly.

Mayonnaise—I can't be bothered making my own mayonnaise at home so I always have a good-quality one on hand. I like using it to make flavored aiolis and tartar sauces and to add a creamy consistency to some vinaigrettes.

Mustard—This is my favorite condiment, hands down. I always have a good-quality Dijon and stone-ground mustard in my fridge.

Olives—I go for green ones such as picholine and black types including Kalamata and Niçoise.

Peppers and fresh chiles—Fresh chiles, bell peppers, and piquillos can add so much flavor to so many things. I prefer using red or yellow bell peppers over green and always have a few jalapeño, serrano, or habanero chiles hanging around to spice up any dish. Piquillos, a variety of Spanish peppers, come roasted and jarred or canned and have an intense flavor all their own.

asparagus

Perfectly Grilled Asparagus • Grilled Asparagus with Green Peppercorn Vinaigrette • Grilled Asparagus with Extra-Virgin Olive Oil, Feta Cheese, and Black Pepper • Grilled Asparagus Wrapped in Prosciutto with Mint Pesto • Grilled Asparagus Chopped Salad with Creamy Meyer Lemon Vinaigrette and Grilled Pita Chip Croutons • Asparagus Vinaigrette • Grilled Asparagus with Grilled Tomato–Tarragon Vinaigrette and Hard-Boiled Eggs • Grilled Asparagus Panzanella • Marinated Grilled Asparagus with Spicy Sesame Vinaigrette • Grilled Flatbread Pizza with Asparagus Pesto and Fontina

Asparagus, with its delicate tapered stalks, is practically the definition of an elegant vegetable. While there's nothing difficult in its preparation, asparagus lends a touch of class to any table. Generally delicate when thin and more robust when thick, asparagus has a distinct, "green" flavor. If you've disliked it in the past, chances are it was overcooked. Try it grilled until just crisp-tender; it will be sweet and wonderful.

Although it is now available year-round, asparagus was traditionally a delicacy marking spring's arrival. I still prefer to eat it fresh from the farmer's market from March through May. Out-of-season asparagus can be slightly bitter and woody through the stalk. Just take a little extra care in your selection and trimming, however, and you should be able to get good results any time of year.

Asparagus is almost always green, but you may encounter both purple and white stalks from time to time. White asparagus is grown entirely underground, never seeing the sun and never producing green chlorophyll. Its flavor runs a bit milder than green asparagus, while the purple is the sweetest of them all.

Asparagus stalks are usually thin in the early spring, getting thicker as its season progresses. One is not necessarily better than the other, however. What matters is freshness, not size. Always choose stalks with tightly closed buds at the tip and avoid stalks whose bottoms look dried out. When it's time to trim, bend the stalk near its base to see where it naturally snaps off. While I think this takes off more than necessary, you can use one test stalk as a guide for trimming the rest of the bunch with a paring knife. You can also peel the stalks if you prefer, especially when using them for the Asparagus Pesto (page 20) to make for a smoother, less fibrous puree.

Perfectly Grilled Asparagus

Serves 4

1½ pounds (about 24 medium stalks) fresh asparagus

3 tablespoons olive oil
Kosher salt and freshly ground black pepper

1. Heat your grill to high.

2. To trim the asparagus, snap the spears with two hands; the tough part should break right off. For a cleaner look and less waste, you can cut off the tough bottoms with a knife and peel the bottom half of the stalk if necessary.

3. Place the asparagus on a baking sheet, toss with the oil, and season with salt and pepper. Grill the asparagus, perpendicular to the grates of the grill, for 3 to 5 minutes on each side or until just crisp-tender.

Grilled Asparagus with Green Peppercorn Vinaigrette

Green peppercorns are really wonderful in this light vinaigrette, which finds the right balance of being truly flavorful without being overly assertive. I serve this as a side dish at my restaurant Bar Americain, where it is a customer favorite.

Serves 4

3 tablespoons white wine vinegar
2 teaspoons Dijon mustard
2 teaspoons honey
½ teaspoon kosher salt
¼ teaspoon freshly ground black pepper

¼ cup plus 2 tablespoons extra-virgin olive oil
1 tablespoon green peppercorns in brine, drained
Perfectly Grilled Asparagus (above)

1. Whisk together the vinegar, mustard, honey, salt, and pepper in a small bowl until combined. Slowly whisk in the olive oil until emulsified and then stir in the peppercorns. Let the vinaigrette sit at room temperature for 15 minutes before serving. Alternatively, the vinaigrette can be made up to 8 hours in advance and refrigerated. Bring to room temperature before serving.

2. Transfer the asparagus from the grill to a large platter. Drizzle the vinaigrette over the top and serve immediately.

Grilled Asparagus with Extra-Virgin Olive Oil, Feta Cheese, and Black Pepper

Is it their long, skinny, spaghetti-like shape that makes me think of pasta when dressing asparagus? Who knows? Regardless, this simple combination of asparagus, pepper, cheese, and herbaceous olive oil is delicious. Feta has a sharp bite that's heightened by the black pepper, and the olive oil keeps it luscious.

Serves 4

Perfectly Grilled Asparagus (page 11)
6 tablespoons extra-virgin olive oil
1 teaspoon coarsely ground black pepper

½ teaspoon kosher salt
6 ounces feta cheese, crumbled

Transfer the asparagus from the grill to a large platter. Add the oil, pepper, and salt and toss to combine. Top the asparagus with the feta and serve immediately.

Grilled Asparagus Wrapped in Prosciutto with Mint Pesto

Grilled food can definitely be elevated above the picnic table, and this dish is a wonderful example. These elegant bundles can be served as a starter, side dish, or salad course. I love to pair mint with savory foods, and the bright freshness of the pesto is a perfect foil for the salty prosciutto. See photograph on page 8.

Serves 4 to 6

½ cup packed fresh mint leaves
1 cup packed fresh flat-leaf parsley leaves
1 clove garlic
3 tablespoons chopped walnuts
¼ cup plus 1 tablespoon extra-virgin olive oil
3 tablespoons freshly grated
  Parmigiano-Reggiano

Kosher salt and freshly ground black
  pepper
Perfectly Grilled Asparagus (page 11)
4 paper-thin slices prosciutto, cut in half
  crosswise
2 teaspoons grated lemon zest

1. Put the mint, parsley, garlic, and walnuts in a food processor and process until coarsely chopped. With the motor running, slowly add the oil and process until smooth. Add 2 tablespoons of the cheese and pulse a few times to combine. Season with salt and pepper. The pesto can be made up to 4 hours in advance, covered, and refrigerated.

2. Divide the asparagus into 8 bundles and wrap each bundle with a slice of prosciutto. Place on a platter, drizzle each bundle with some of the pesto, and garnish with the lemon zest and remaining cheese. Serve warm or at room temperature.

Grilled Asparagus Chopped Salad with Creamy Meyer Lemon Vinaigrette and Grilled Pita Chip Croutons

I have had this beautiful salad on the menu at my restaurant Bar Americain since the day it opened and it still continues to be one of the most popular dishes. If you can get your hands on fresh Meyer lemons during their season from November to January, use them for this vinaigrette. If they are not available, simply use three parts fresh lemon juice to one part fresh orange juice as a substitute in the vinaigrette. A Meyer lemon is thought to be a cross between a lemon and a mandarin orange.

Serves 4 to 6

2 pocketless pita breads
Olive oil
Kosher salt and freshly ground black pepper
4 cups mesclun greens
½ pint grape tomatoes, halved
8 ounces aged white Cheddar cheese,
    cut into ½-inch dice

1 English cucumber, cut into ½-inch dice
½ cup black olives, pitted and coarsely chopped
1 cup canned chickpeas, drained, rinsed, and
    drained again
Perfectly Grilled Asparagus (page 11), cut
    into 1-inch pieces
Meyer Lemon Dressing (recipe follows)

1. Heat your grill to high.

2. Brush the pita on both sides with oil and season with salt and pepper. Grill until golden brown and crispy, about 1 minute per side. Remove the pita to a cutting board and cut each pita in half. Cut each half into ½-inch slices.

3. Combine the mesclun, tomatoes, cheese, cucumber, olives, chickpeas, and asparagus in a large bowl. Add half of the dressing and toss well to coat; season with salt and pepper. Drizzle with more of the dressing and top with the pita chips.

14

Meyer Lemon Dressing

Makes approximately ¾ cup

¼ cup fresh Meyer lemon juice or 3 tablespoons fresh lemon juice plus 1 tablespoon fresh orange juice
1 tablespoon red wine vinegar
2 teaspoons honey
1 tablespoon mayonnaise

2 teaspoons Dijon mustard
1 teaspoon whole-grain mustard
Kosher salt and freshly ground black pepper
½ cup extra-virgin olive oil
2 tablespoons chopped fresh tarragon leaves

Whisk together the Meyer lemon juice, vinegar, honey, mayonnaise, both mustards, and salt and pepper to taste in a medium bowl. Slowly whisk in the oil until emulsified and then stir in the tarragon.

Asparagus Vinaigrette

This classic recipe always seems to be made with bottled Italian dressing, which is usually loaded with preservatives and lots of sugar. It's just as easy to prepare a homemade vinaigrette, and the result will be much more flavorful. This recipe is perfect to take along on picnics and can be made a couple days in advance because the longer it sits, the better it tastes.

Serves 4

3 tablespoons white wine vinegar
1 tablespoon fresh lemon juice
1 teaspoon honey
2 cloves garlic, finely chopped
2 tablespoons finely chopped fresh flat-leaf parsley leaves
2 teaspoons finely chopped fresh oregano leaves

¼ teaspoon red chile flakes
½ teaspoon kosher salt
¼ teaspoon freshly ground black pepper
½ extra-virgin cup olive oil
Perfectly Grilled Asparagus (page 11)
¼ cup freshly grated Parmigiano-Reggiano

1. Whisk together the vinegar, lemon juice, honey, garlic, parsley, oregano, chile flakes, salt, and pepper in a medium bowl. Slowly whisk in the oil until emulsified.

2. Place the asparagus in a medium baking dish, pour the vinaigrette over, and toss to coat. Cover and refrigerate for at least 30 minutes and up to 2 days before serving. Sprinkle with the cheese just before serving.

Grilled Asparagus with Grilled Tomato–Tarragon Vinaigrette and Hard-Boiled Eggs

Asparagus and eggs are a classic pairing, whether in a dish of steamed asparagus with *sauce gribiche* or in the brunch favorite eggs Benedict with asparagus. Asparagus and anise-flavored tarragon are both strong, distinctive tastes that stand up to—but do not overpower—one another.

Serves 4

¼ cup balsamic vinegar
2 cloves garlic, finely chopped
1 tablespoon finely chopped fresh tarragon leaves, plus more leaves for garnish
Kosher salt and freshly ground black pepper

¼ cup plus 2 tablespoons extra-virgin olive oil
3 ripe plum tomatoes
½ small red onion, thinly sliced
Perfectly Grilled Asparagus (page 11)
4 hard-boiled eggs (see note), thinly sliced

1. Heat your grill to high.

2. Whisk together the vinegar, garlic, tarragon, and salt and pepper to taste in a medium bowl. Slowly whisk in the ¼ cup olive oil until emulsified. Let the vinaigrette sit at room temperature while you grill the tomatoes.

3. Brush the tomatoes with the remaining 2 tablespoons olive oil and season with salt and pepper. Grill the tomatoes until blackened on all sides, 2 to 3 minutes per side.

4. Remove the tomatoes from the grill and let cool slightly. When cool enough to handle, cut the tomatoes in half crosswise and remove the seeds. Cut the tomato halves into small dice and place in the bowl with the vinaigrette. Add the onion and season with salt and pepper. Let the vinaigrette sit at room temperature for at least 15 minutes before serving. Alternatively, the vinaigrette can be made 8 hours in advance and refrigerated. Bring to room temperature before using.

5. Place the grilled asparagus on a large platter and spoon the vinaigrette over the top. Top with the sliced eggs and tarragon leaves.

To hard-boil eggs

Place the eggs in a small saucepan, cover with cold water, and bring to a boil over high heat on the stove or grates of the grill. Cover, remove from the heat, and let stand for 15 minutes. Drain the eggs, cover with cold water, and let sit for 5 minutes; drain again. Use immediately or cover and refrigerate for up to 3 days.

Grilled Asparagus Panzanella

The thrifty Italians may have invented panzanella as a way to use up stale bread, but I buy bread and put it out for the sole purpose of making this hearty salad. Grilled asparagus adds another dimension to the play of sweet cherry tomatoes and basil with briny olives and capers.

Serves 4 to 6

6 (1-inch) slices day-old country-style bread
¼ cup red wine vinegar
2 cloves garlic, finely chopped
Kosher salt and freshly ground black pepper
½ cup extra-virgin olive oil
Perfectly Grilled Asparagus (page 11), cut into
   1-inch pieces

8 red cherry tomatoes, quartered
8 yellow cherry tomatoes, quartered
1 small red onion, halved and thinly sliced
½ cup Niçoise olives, pitted
2 tablespoons capers, drained
8 fresh basil leaves, cut into thin ribbons,
   plus more leaves for garnish

1. Heat your grill to high.

2. Grill the bread on both sides until slightly charred, about 1 minute per side. Remove from the grill and cut each slice into 1-inch cubes.

3. Whisk together the vinegar, garlic, ½ teaspoon salt, ¼ teaspoon pepper, and the oil in a large bowl until combined. Add the asparagus, red and yellow tomatoes, onion, olives, capers, grilled bread, and basil and mix until combined. Season with salt and pepper. Let sit at room temperature for at least 30 minutes and up to 1 hour before serving.

Marinated Grilled Asparagus
with Spicy Sesame Vinaigrette

I love cold crisp asparagus just as much as I like hot-off-the-grill asparagus. This is a perfect recipe to take on a picnic. Serve alongside Three-Chile Glazed Grilled Tuna (page 253).

Serves 4

¼ cup rice vinegar
2 teaspoons honey
1 tablespoon Asian hot chile/garlic sauce, such as Sriracha, or 1 teaspoon red chile flakes and 1 finely chopped clove garlic
1 tablespoon low-sodium soy sauce
2 teaspoons toasted sesame oil

¼ teaspoon kosher salt
¼ teaspoon freshly ground black pepper
¼ cup canola oil
2 tablespoons white sesame seeds, toasted (see note)
Perfectly Grilled Asparagus (page 11)

1. Whisk together the vinegar, honey, chile sauce, soy sauce, sesame oil, salt, pepper, canola oil, and sesame seeds until combined.

2. Place the grilled asparagus in a baking dish, pour the vinaigrette over, and turn to coat. Cover and refrigerate for at least 4 hours and up to 24 hours before serving.

To toast seeds or nuts

Put a single layer of seeds or nuts in a sauté pan and toast over medium-low heat (either on the grates of the grill or on the stovetop), shaking the pan every couple of minutes to prevent burning, until lightly golden brown and fragrant, 5 to 7 minutes. Transfer to a plate and let cool completely.

Grilled Flatbread Pizza with Asparagus Pesto and Fontina

This flatbread pizza is a wonderful option for a satisfying vegetarian appetizer or main course. Grilling asparagus intensifies its already pronounced flavor and gives this pesto a slightly smoky taste. Asparagus, basil, and lemon are a match made in heaven and one that works especially well here as the bright, acidic lemon and sweet and herbaceous basil keep the asparagus-based pesto tasting fresh.

For this particular recipe it is best to use the thinnest asparagus stalks you can find and to overcook them ever so slightly to make the smoothest pesto. To achieve this without turning the asparagus gray, remove the asparagus from the grill, place them on a platter, wrap tightly with plastic wrap, and let them steam for 10 minutes before proceeding with the pesto recipe.

Serves 4 to 6

1¼ pounds asparagus, cooked as for Perfectly Grilled Asparagus (page 11), coarsely chopped
½ cup packed fresh basil leaves, plus more leaves for garnish
Grated zest of 2 lemons
2 cloves garlic, chopped

2 tablespoons pine nuts
¾ cup plus 2 tablespoons olive oil
Kosher salt and freshly ground black pepper
¾ cup freshly grated Pecorino Romano cheese
Flatbreads (recipe follows) or 2 (8-inch) prepared pizza shells (such as Boboli)
1 pound fontina cheese, thinly sliced

1. Heat your grill to high.

2. Combine 1 pound of the asparagus, the basil, lemon zest of 1 lemon, garlic, and pine nuts in a food processor and pulse a few times to coarsely chop. With the motor running, slowly add the ¾ cup extra-virgin olive oil and process until the mixture is smooth; season with salt and pepper. Transfer the pesto to a bowl and stir in ½ cup of the Pecorino Romano cheese.

3. Brush the tops of the flatbreads with the 2 tablespoons olive oil and place oiled side down on the grill. Grill until slightly crisp, about 1 minute. Remove the flatbreads from the grill, turn right side up, and spread each with the pesto. Top with the fontina and the remaining ¼ pound of asparagus. Return the pizzas to the grill, close the cover, and continue cooking until the cheese has melted, 2 to 3 minutes.

4. Remove the pizzas from the grill and sprinkle with the remaining ¼ cup Pecorino Romano cheese and lemon zest. Garnish with basil leaves. Cut into slices and serve immediately.

Flatbreads

Makes 2 (8-inch) flatbreads

¾ cup warm water (105 to 115 degrees F)
1 teaspoon active dry yeast
6 tablespoons olive oil

2 cups all-purpose flour, plus more for
 rolling
1 teaspoon kosher salt

1. Mix the water and yeast in a medium bowl and let stand for 5 minutes until foamy. Add 2 tablespoons of the olive oil, the flour, and salt and stir until combined.

2. Transfer the mixture to a lightly floured flat surface and knead until the texture of the dough is smooth. Grease the bottom and sides of a large bowl with 1 tablespoon of the remaining olive oil. Add the dough and turn to coat in the oil. Cover with a cloth and place in warm place until doubled in size, about 1 hour.

3. Heat your grill to high.

4. Gently press on the dough to release some of the air and transfer to a lightly floured surface. Divide the dough into 2 equal pieces and roll each into an 8-inch circle. Brush the tops with 1½ tablespoons of the olive oil, place on the grill, and cook until golden brown and lightly charred on the bottom, 3 to 4 minutes. Brush the top side of the flat breads with the remaining 1½ tablespoons of olive oil, turn over, and continue grilling until lightly golden brown on the bottom, 2 to 3 minutes longer.

beef

Perfectly Grilled Steak • Grilled Steak with Balsamic-Rosemary Butter • Grilled Rib Eye with Horseradish Sauce • Grilled Filet Mignon with Fig–Cabernet Vinegar Glaze • Spice-Rubbed Rib Eye with Bar Americain Steak Sauce • Red Wine–Marinated Flank Steak Filled with Prosciutto, Fontina, and Basil • Spanish Spice–Rubbed Steak with Sherry Vinegar Steak Sauce • Mini Open-Faced Steak Sandwiches on Garlic Bread with Aged Provolone, Caramelized Onions, and Parsley Oil • Thai-Inspired Grilled Beef Salad with Watercress • Santa Maria–Style BBQ Tri Tip

There is something so satisfying about beef; it's hard for me to turn down a steak when my hunger is kicked up into full gear. And when it's prepared on the grill, the pleasure it gives is practically primal. Charred and crusty on the outside with a juicy interior, a well-grilled steak is a great thing.

From your local supermarket to the specialty butcher, you can find a plethora of cuts and grades of beef readily available these days. Options range from organic grass-fed to kosher to the trendy Kobe-style beef. Most beef in this country is raised on a diet of grass until the last few months, when it is fattened up with grains, primarily corn. This beef tends to be milder in flavor and fattier than purely grass-fed beef. Grass-fed beef has a slightly more pronounced "beefy" flavor. Most American palates are accustomed to the flavor of grain-fed beef, but grass-fed is certainly worth trying if you come across it. What it all comes down to, though, is flavor, and you can find and emphasize that in any cut and/or style.

Beef is graded on its marbling: the more marbling, the better. Those ribbons of fat running through beef melt during cooking and create endless flavor and juiciness. It might not look as pretty as that lean, red steak, but adequate marbling is the key to a superior end result. While in better restaurants and butcher shops you are likely to see meat that has been labeled prime, only a small percentage of beef has enough marbling to qualify as such. Supermarket beef is generally labeled choice, the most popular and available grade. I like to use dry-aged prime beef at home and in my restaurants, but it can be pricey and hard to find. You can achieve good results with choice as well. Just be sure to look for some marbling and remember, the less fat your cut has, the less you should cook it.

A very lean cut won't have enough fat to stay juicy if you cook it past medium. This is the case with the super-lean tenderloin. Tenderloin is certainly supple, but it doesn't have a very full beefy flavor on its own, which is why I like to punch it up with rubs. A rub will also help create a beautiful crusty exterior, making a differentiation in textures that the meat might not have on its own. There are other cuts that you won't want to cook past medium or medium rare, such as skirt and flank steaks. These are plenty flavorful and juicy, but they have a pronounced grain that becomes tough if overcooked. Marinades are popular treatments for these cuts as they break down some of those tough fibers, but cooking flank and skirt steaks quickly and then cutting thin across the grain will also ensure a tasty, juicy, slightly chewy steak—not a tough one.

Here's a cooking tip for beef—especially if you like your meat as I do, cooked to a nice medium-rare (or medium): Pull your meat out of the refrigerator about twenty minutes before you plan on grilling it. You want it to come to room temperature so that it grills at an even, level rate. This way you won't char the outside before the inside loses its icy chill.

There is one other thing that I cannot stress enough when it comes to grilling beef—or most any meat for that matter: Let it rest! Pulling your meat off of the grill and then letting it sit for five minutes or so under a foil tent is incredibly important. Give those precious juices time to settle back into the meat. Cut the meat too soon and all of those juices will run off into the cutting board, right where you don't want them.

Perfectly Grilled Steak

The grill might just be about the best thing to happen to a steak, and vice versa. There isn't much that tastes better than a simply grilled, crusty-on-the-outside, juicy-on-the-inside steak. For a perfect steak, grill it over high heat and don't touch it! As tempting as it may be to spear and flip your steak repeatedly, you need to leave it alone until a nice crust forms, pulling the meat away from the grill before you turn it over. After that, it's up to you!

Serves 4

4 (12-ounce) boneless rib-eye or New York strip steaks or filets mignons

2 tablespoons canola or olive oil
Kosher salt and freshly ground black pepper

1. Twenty minutes before grilling, remove the steaks from the refrigerator and let sit, covered, at room temperature.

2. Heat your grill to high.

3. Brush the steaks on both sides with oil and season liberally with salt and pepper. Place the steaks on the grill and let cook until golden brown and slightly charred, 4 to 5 minutes. Turn the steaks over and continue grilling for 5 to 6 minutes for medium-rare (an internal temperature of 135 degrees F), 7 to 8 minutes for medium (140 degrees F), or 9 to 10 minutes for medium-well (150 degrees F).

4. Remove the steaks to a cutting board or platter, tent loosely with foil, and let rest for 5 minutes before slicing.

Grilled Steak with Balsamic-Rosemary Butter

A dab or two of herbed butter does wonderful things to simply grilled steak, infusing it with flavor and extra richness. The combination of these two Italian favored ingredients makes a big impression as the butter melts into the steak, lending balsamic's sweet tang and rosemary's piney note to every delicious bite. A butter such as this one is an easy way to add a touch of decadence and sophisticated flavor to any grilled steak.

Serves 4

2 cups balsamic vinegar
2 teaspoons whole black peppercorns
2 teaspoons honey
2 tablespoons chopped fresh rosemary leaves
   plus sprigs for garnish

12 tablespoons (1½ sticks) unsalted butter,
   slightly softened
1 teaspoon kosher salt
Perfectly Grilled Steak (page 25)

1. Combine the vinegar and peppercorns in a small saucepan over high heat and cook, stirring occasionally, until reduced to ¼ cup, 8 to 10 minutes. Remove the peppercorns, whisk in the honey and rosemary, and let cool to room temperature.

2. Combine the balsamic mixture with the butter and salt in a food processor and process until smooth. Scrape into a bowl and refrigerate for 30 minutes to set slightly. The balsamic-rosemary butter can be made 1 day in advance and stored, covered, in the refrigerator. Remove from the refrigerator 15 minutes before serving.

3. Top each steak with a few tablespoons of the butter and garnish with rosemary sprigs, if desired.

Grilled Rib Eye with Horseradish Sauce

Every year around Christmastime, I get this yearning for a perfectly roasted prime rib, studded with garlic, with all the classic fixin's—such as Yorkshire pudding and horseradish sauce. I haven't figured out a way to do Yorkshire pudding on the grill, but I can sure grill up a garlicky steak and serve it with a horseradish sauce (one that requires no cooking at all) to satisfy that craving—any time of year!

Serves 4

4 (12-ounce) boneless rib-eye steaks
½ cup olive oil
3 cloves garlic
Kosher salt and freshly ground black pepper

1 cup crème fraîche or sour cream
6 tablespoons prepared horseradish, drained
¼ cup finely chopped fresh chives

1. Twenty minutes before grilling, remove the steaks from the refrigerator and let sit, covered, at room temperature.

2. Meanwhile, combine the oil and garlic in a small saucepan and season with salt and pepper. Heat over low heat for 2 minutes. Remove from the heat and let sit for 15 minutes.

3. Heat your grill to high.

4. Whisk together the crème fraîche, horseradish, chives, ½ teaspoon salt, and ¼ teaspoon pepper in a small bowl. Cover and refrigerate while you grill the steaks.

5. Brush the steaks on both sides with the garlic oil and season liberally with salt and pepper. Place the steaks on the grill and let cook, brushing with the oil every minute or so, until golden brown and slightly charred, 4 to 5 minutes. Turn the steaks over and continue grilling for 5 to 6 minutes for medium-rare.

6. Remove the steaks to a cutting board or platter, tent loosely with foil, and let rest for 5 minutes before slicing. Serve with the horseradish sauce on the side.

Grilled Filet Mignon with Fig–Cabernet Vinegar Glaze

With flavors ranging from sweet to tart to tangy to fruity, these vinegars have so many uses beyond vinaigrettes. Cabernet vinegar is made from cabernet wine that has been fermented and then aged in oak barrels. The robust flavor is perfect for adding to sauces and glazes and pairs beautifully with red meat.

Serves 4

5 tablespoons olive oil
3 shallots, finely chopped
2 cups cabernet vinegar or other red wine vinegar
1 cup dry red wine, preferably cabernet
6 dried figs
1 tablespoon chopped fresh thyme leaves, plus whole sprigs for garnish

2 tablespoons honey
Kosher salt
½ teaspoon coarsely ground black pepper
4 (8-ounce) filets mignons
Freshly ground black pepper
8 fresh figs, halved

1. Heat 1 tablespoon of the oil in a medium saucepan over high heat. Add the shallots and cook until lightly golden brown. Add the vinegar, red wine, dried figs, and thyme and cook, stirring occasionally, until the figs are soft and the liquid is reduced by half, 15 to 20 minutes.

2. Transfer the mixture to a food processor and process until smooth. Wipe out the pan, strain the mixture back into the pan, and place over high heat. Cook until the mixture is thickened, 5 to 7 minutes. Stir in the honey and season with ½ teaspoon salt and the coarse black pepper. Let cool.

3. Twenty minutes before grilling, remove the steaks from the refrigerator and let sit, covered, at room temperature.

4. Heat your grill to high.

5. Brush both sides of the filets with 2 tablespoons of the oil and season with salt and freshly ground black pepper. Place on the grill and grill until golden brown and slightly charred, 4 to 5 minutes. Turn the steaks over and continue grilling until cooked to medium-rare, 3 to 4 minutes.

6. Transfer the steaks to a platter and immediately spoon some of the glaze over each steak. Tent with foil and let rest for 5 minutes.

7. While the steaks are resting, brush the fresh figs on both sides with the remaining 2 tablespoons oil. Grill the figs until they are soft and lightly browned, about 2 minutes per side.

8. Uncover the steaks, top with the figs, and garnish with thyme before serving.

Spice-Rubbed Rib Eye with Bar Americain Steak Sauce

The steak sauce at Bar Americain is, if I do say so myself, so good. It gets a complex, deep note of sweetness from molasses and honey and a nice sharp bite and popping texture from the mixture of whole-grain and Dijon mustards; and horseradish, which we all love with steak, gives it a familiar heat. Now, don't worry that this dish will be too spicy, even with the quarter cup of ancho chile powder in the steak rub. Ancho chiles have a taste that I compare to a spicy raisin, and the rest of the rub's ingredients come together to create a smoky, savory, and mouth-wateringly delicious steak. You'll enjoy each and every last bite, no fire extinguishers needed.

Serves 4

¼ cup ancho chile powder
1½ tablespoons sweet paprika
2 teaspoons dried oregano
2 teaspoons ground coriander
2 teaspoons dry mustard
1 tablespoon plus 2 teaspoons kosher salt

2 teaspoons freshly ground black pepper
1 teaspoon ground cumin
4 (12-ounce) boneless rib-eye steaks
2 tablespoons canola oil
Bar Americain Steak Sauce (recipe follows)

1. Whisk together the ancho, paprika, oregano, coriander, mustard, 2 teaspoons of the salt, the pepper, and the cumin in a small bowl.

2. Twenty minutes before grilling, remove the steaks from the refrigerator and let sit, covered, at room temperature.

3. Heat your grill to high.

4. Brush the steaks on both sides with the oil and season with the remaining 1 tablespoon salt. Rub 1 side of each steak with the spice rub and place on the grill, rub side down. Grill until golden brown and slightly charred, 3 to 4 minutes. Flip the steaks over, close the cover of the grill, and continue cooking for 5 to 6 minutes for medium-rare.

5. Remove the steaks to a cutting board or platter, tent loosely with foil, and let rest for 5 minutes. Serve with Bar Americain steak sauce on the side.

Bar Americain Steak Sauce

Makes approximately 1 cup

¼ cup Dijon mustard
¼ cup whole-grain mustard
¼ cup molasses
2 tablespoons ketchup

2 tablespoons honey
1 tablespoon prepared horseradish, drained
½ teaspoon kosher salt
¼ teaspoon freshly ground black pepper

Whisk together both of the mustards, the molasses, ketchup, honey, horseradish, salt, and pepper in a small bowl. Cover and refrigerate for at least 30 minutes or up to 1 day. Bring to room temperature before serving.

Red Wine–Marinated Flank Steak Filled with Prosciutto, Fontina, and Basil

You can't help but impress when serving this dish. The Italian stuffing loads the already flavorful flank steak with an enticing, beautifully melted blend of fresh basil, salty prosciutto, and nutty fontina cheese. Redolent of both onions and garlic yet sweeter and milder than both, shallots are a favorite ingredient of mine and I utilize them here in both a red wine reduction and the marinade. Be sure to use a wine you like enough to drink for the reduction, as cooking it only intensifies its flavor.

Serves 4 to 6

4 shallots, coarsely chopped
1 cup dry red wine
¼ cup plus 2 tablespoons olive oil
1 (2-pound) flank steak, butterflied
Kosher salt and freshly ground black pepper

4 ounces thinly sliced prosciutto
4 ounces thinly sliced fontina cheese
14 fresh basil leaves, plus more leaves for garnish
Cabernet-Shallot Reduction (recipe follows)

1. Whisk together the shallots, wine, and ¼ cup of the olive oil in a large baking dish. Add the steak and turn to coat. Cover and refrigerate for at least 4 hours or overnight.

2. Heat your grill to high.

3. Remove the steak from the marinade and blot with paper towels. Lay on a flat surface, cut side up, and season with salt and pepper. Cover the surface with the prosciutto slices, then top with the cheese and a layer of the basil leaves. Starting with one of the long sides, tightly roll up the steak around the filling. Using kitchen string, tie the roll in 4 or 5 places.

4. Brush the outside of the steak with the remaining 2 tablespoons of oil and season with salt and pepper. Grill the steak over high heat until browned all over, 8 to 10 minutes, turning the steak 4 times as it cooks. Move the meat to a cooler part of the grill, away from the direct heat, and grill for 15 to 20 minutes, or until an instant-read thermometer inserted into the meat registers 120 to 125 degrees F for medium-rare.

5. Transfer the steak to a platter, tent loosely with foil, and let rest for 5 minutes before slicing. Slice against the grain into ½-inch-thick slices, drizzle with the red wine reduction, and garnish with basil leaves.

Cabernet-Shallot Reduction

Makes 1 cup

2 teaspoons olive oil
3 shallots, finely chopped
1 (750-ml) bottle cabernet wine

1 teaspoon black peppercorns
2 tablespoons honey
Kosher salt

1. Heat the oil in a large saucepan on the grates of the grill or on the stovetop over high heat. Add the shallots and cook until soft, about 2 minutes. Add the wine and peppercorns, bring to a boil, and cook until the wine thickens and has reduced to 1 cup, about 12 to 15 minutes.

2. Strain the mixture into a bowl, add the honey, and season with salt. The reduction can be made 1 day in advance and kept refrigerated. Reheat before serving.

Spanish Spice–Rubbed Steak with Sherry Vinegar Steak Sauce

I serve this steak at my Spanish-inspired restaurant, Bolo, where it is a perennial favorite. The rub is slightly smoky but not hot—really savory and tasty. And as for the sherry vinegar steak sauce, it's so incredibly delicious you'll want to smother every bite in it. Sherry vinegar has a sweet-sour taste that manages to be both mellow and acidic; it's really worth seeking out. I think that no steak sauce is complete without a little horseradish bite, and molasses and honey round out the sharp flavors with their deep sweetness.

Serves 4

3 tablespoons Spanish paprika
2 teaspoons ground cumin
2 teaspoons dry mustard
2 teaspoons ground fennel seeds
Kosher salt and coarsely ground black pepper

4 (12-ounce) boneless rib-eye or New York
   strip steaks or filets mignons
2 tablespoons olive oil
Sherry Vinegar Steak Sauce (recipe follows)

1. Whisk together the paprika, cumin, mustard, fennel, 2 teaspoons salt, and 1 teaspoon pepper in a small bowl until combined.

2. Twenty minutes before grilling, remove the steaks from the refrigerator and let sit, covered, at room temperature.

3. Heat your grill to high.

4. Brush the steaks on both sides with oil and season liberally with salt and pepper. Rub 1 side of each steak with about 1 tablespoon of the spice mixture. Place the steaks on the grill, rub side down, and let cook until golden brown and slightly charred, 3 to 4 minutes. Turn the steaks over and continue grilling for 5 to 6 minutes for medium-rare.

5. Remove the steaks to a cutting board or platter, tent loosely with foil, and let rest for 5 minutes before slicing. Serve with the sherry vinegar steak sauce on the side.

Sherry Vinegar Steak Sauce

Makes approximately 1 cup

2 red bell peppers, grilled (see page 120), peeled,
    seeded, and chopped or 6 piquillo peppers,
    chopped
½ cup aged sherry vinegar
3 tablespoons Dijon mustard
2 tablespoons prepared horseradish, drained

2 tablespoons honey
1 tablespoon molasses
2 teaspoons Worcestershire sauce
1 teaspoon kosher salt
½ teaspoon freshly ground black pepper

Combine the bell peppers, vinegar, mustard, horseradish, honey, molasses, Worcestershire, salt, and black pepper in a food processor or blender and blend until
smooth. If the mixture is too thick to pour, add a few tablespoons of water. The sauce
can be made 1 day in advance and refrigerated. Bring to room temperature before
serving.

Mini Open-Faced Steak Sandwiches
on Garlic Bread with Aged Provolone, Caramelized Onions, and Parsley Oil

A Philly cheese steak can be a great way to top off a night out on the town. But what about transforming that cheesy, savory goodness into something far more appropriate for *starting off* your night? I think this upscale Philly cheese steak appetizer is right on the money. Juicy slices of rib-eye steak and sharp provolone cheese take over for the standard beef and processed cheese, and I've upped the flavor ante even more by serving it on crusty garlic bread with a pile of sweet, rich caramelized onions. Parsley oil, fresh and green, is just the right elegant finish for these delectable mini sandwiches.

Serves 4 to 6

1 (16-ounce) boneless rib-eye steak
2 tablespoons olive oil
Kosher salt and freshly ground black pepper
10 tablespoons (1¼ sticks) unsalted butter, at room temperature
6 cloves garlic, roasted (see note, page 38), peeled, and mashed

12 (½-inch-thick) slices French bread
6 (¼-inch-thick) slices aged provolone cheese, halved lengthwise
Caramelized Onions (recipe follows)
Parsley Oil (recipe follows)

1. Twenty minutes before grilling, remove the steak from the refrigerator and let sit, covered, at room temperature.

2. Heat your grill to high.

3. Brush the steak on both sides with the oil and season with salt and pepper. Place on the grill and cook until golden brown and slightly charred, 4 to 5 minutes. Turn over and continue grilling for 6 to 7 minutes for medium-rare.

4. Transfer the steak to a cutting board, tent loosely with foil, and let rest for 5 minutes. Slice into ¼-inch-thick slices.

5. While the steak is resting, mix together the butter and garlic puree and season with salt and pepper. Brush 1 side of each slice of bread with 1 tablespoon of the butter and place on the grill, butter side down. Grill until golden brown, 1 to 2 minutes, turn over, top with the cheese, and grill for 30 seconds longer or until the cheese melts.

6. Place the garlic bread on a platter and top with some of the caramelized onions and a few thin slices of the beef. Drizzle with the parsley oil.

(continued)

Caramelized Onions

Makes 1¼ cups

2 tablespoons olive oil
2 tablespoons unsalted butter
3 large Spanish onions, peeled, halved, and
  thinly sliced

1 tablespoon balsamic vinegar
Kosher salt and freshly ground black pepper

Heat the oil and butter in a large sauté pan on the grates of the grill or on a stovetop over medium heat. Add the onions and cook, stirring occasionally, until soft and caramelized, 35 to 40 minutes. Add the vinegar and season with salt and pepper. The onions can be covered and refrigerated for up to 1 day. Reheat before serving.

Parsley Oil

Makes ½ cup

¼ cup finely chopped fresh flat-leaf parsley
  leaves

½ cup extra-virgin olive oil
Kosher salt and freshly ground black pepper

Mix together the parsley and oil in a small bowl and season with salt and pepper. The parsley oil can be covered and refrigerated overnight. Bring to room temperature before serving.

To roast garlic

Heat your grill to medium or preheat the oven to 300 degrees F. Separate the cloves of a head of garlic but do not peel them. Put the cloves on a square of heavy duty aluminum foil, drizzle with 1 tablespoon olive oil, and season with salt and pepper. Wrap the garlic in the foil and put on the grates of the grill or in the oven. Close the grill cover and cook for 45 minutes to 1 hour until the garlic is very soft. Remove from the heat. When the garlic is cool enough to handle, squeeze the pulp out of the skins. Roasted garlic can be covered and refrigerated for up to 3 days.

Thai-Inspired Grilled Beef Salad with Watercress

Great for a luncheon or a light dinner, this salad is fresh and satisfying. I call this dish Thai *inspired,* for while you will find beef salads on many Thai menus this recipe is not quite the traditional preparation. Also, I like to add watercress in place of noodles, which makes what was a starter into a heartier main course salad.

Serves 4

Marinated Beef

¼ cup hoisin sauce
2 tablespoons hot chile sauce (such as Sriracha)
3 tablespoons rice wine vinegar
2 tablespoons fresh lime juice
2 tablespoons toasted sesame oil
6 cloves garlic, coarsely chopped
1 (2-inch) piece fresh ginger, peeled and coarsely chopped
1½ pounds beef tenderloin
Kosher salt and freshly ground black pepper

Salad

3 tablespoons rice wine vinegar
2 tablespoons low-sodium soy sauce
1 tablespoon fresh lime juice
1 tablespoon honey
¼ cup canola oil
3 tablespoons chopped fresh cilantro leaves, plus more for garnish
Kosher salt and freshly ground black pepper
5 cups chopped watercress
1 cup shredded carrots
3 green onions, thinly sliced
¼ cup packed fresh basil leaves
¼ cup packed fresh mint leaves

1. To marinate the beef, whisk together the hoisin, chile sauce, vinegar, lime juice, sesame oil, garlic, and ginger in a medium baking dish. Add the beef and turn to coat in the mixture. Cover and let marinate in the refrigerator for at least 2 hours and up to 8 hours.

2. Twenty minutes before grilling, remove the beef from the refrigerator and from the marinade and place on a plate. Cover and let sit at room temperature.

3. Heat your grill to high.

4. Grill the meat until golden brown and slightly charred on all sides and cooked to medium-rare, 10 to 12 minutes. Transfer to a cutting board; tent loosely with foil, and let rest for 5 minutes before slicing into ¼-inch-thick slices.

5. While the meat is resting, combine the vinegar, soy sauce, lime juice, honey, canola oil, and cilantro in a blender and blend until smooth. Season with salt and pepper. Combine the watercress, carrots, green onions, basil, and mint in a large bowl and toss with the vinaigrette.

6. Transfer the salad to a platter, top with the steak, and garnish with cilantro leaves.

Santa Maria–Style BBQ Tri Tip

If you are not from coastal California, you may not be familiar with the tri tip cut of beef. Let me tell you, it makes for one delicious steak. Here the tri tip (your butcher should be able to get this for you if it's not carried in your local store) is rubbed with a simple but savory blend of salt, pepper, and garlic salt and then grilled to perfection. Carved into tender slices, it is just about always served with a simple but hearty bean relish, and I'm not one to mess with tradition—at least in this case! Mixed with smoky bacon, fresh herbs, garlic, onion, and poblano chile, the bean relish adds a nice kick of flavor and another layer of texture to this excellent dish. Tomato relish completes the dish with its freshness. You've got to do what they do in Santa Maria, though, and serve this up alongside big slices of grilled French bread to sop up all of those awesome juices.

Serves 4 to 6

Tri Tip Steak

2 tablespoons kosher salt
1 tablespoon garlic salt
1 tablespoon coarsely ground black pepper
1 (2½-pound) tri tip roast, fat trimmed
2 tablespoons canola oil
Tomato Relish (recipe follows)

Santa Maria Pinquito Bean Relish

8 ounces bacon, finely diced
1 medium Spanish onion, finely diced
1 poblano chile, finely diced
2 cloves garlic, finely chopped
2 (15.5-ounce) cans pinquito or pinto beans,
  drained, rinsed, and drained again
2 tablespoons chopped cilantro or flat-leaf parsley
Kosher salt and freshly ground black pepper

1. Heat your grill to high

2. To grill the steak, combine the salt, garlic salt, and pepper in a small bowl. Rub the mixture all over the beef and drizzle with the oil. Put the steak on the grill and cook, turning once, until golden brown and slightly charred on both sides and cooked to medium-rare, about 15 minutes total.

3. Meanwhile, make the bean relish. Heat a large sauté pan over the grates of the grill or on a stovetop over medium heat. Add the bacon and cook until golden brown and the fat has rendered, about 10 minutes. Remove the bacon with a slotted spoon to a plate lined with paper towels.

4. Add the onion and poblano to the bacon fat in the pan and cook until soft, 3 to 4 minutes. Add the garlic and cook for 30 seconds. Add the beans and cook until warmed through, 3 to 4 minutes. Fold in the cooked bacon and cilantro, season with salt and pepper, and transfer to a medium bowl.

5. Transfer the steak to a cutting board, tent with foil, and let rest for 5 minutes before slicing across the grain into ¼-inch-thick slices.

6. Spoon the bean relish onto plates, top with the steak, and garnish with a dollop of tomato relish.

Tomato Relish

Makes approximately 2 cups

3 medium ripe beefsteak tomatoes, finely diced
½ small red onion, finely diced
2 cloves garlic, finely chopped
1 serrano or jalapeño chile, finely diced

3 tablespoons olive oil
2 tablespoons chopped fresh flat-leaf parsley or
  cilantro leaves
Kosher salt and freshly ground black pepper

Combine the tomatoes, onion, garlic, chile, olive oil, parsley, and salt and pepper to taste in a medium bowl. Let sit at room temperature for up to 30 minutes before serving.

burgers

Green Chile Cheeseburgers • Texas Burger • Spicy Buffalo-Style Burger with Celery-Carrot Slaw and Blue Cheese Dressing • Blue Cheese Sirloin Burgers with Red Wine–Onion Jam • Nacho Burger • Pressed Burger with Manchego, Serrano Ham, and Piquillo-Smoked Paprika Aioli • Buffalo Burger with Swiss Cheese, Red Cabbage Slaw, and Pickled Okra Russian Dressing • Turkey Patty Melt with Grilled Onion Relish • Spiced Turkey Burgers with Apple Raita and Spinach

I'm a burger man, pure and simple. I'd like to think that it doesn't get much better than a juicy beef burger layered with a slice or two of cheese. But you know what? The possibilities for cooking with ground meat are endless, and I'd be remiss in my duties as a griller if I didn't take the time to explore them. And I'm glad I have, because I've opened up to a world of delicious burgers made from turkey and chicken or buffalo, not to mention other savory preparations such as Mediterranean-inspired burgers. Burgers and other chopped meat dishes are perfect informal party food. The chopped meat tends to be less expensive than whole cuts, everyone seems to love burgers, and it's fun to show off the new and exciting ways you have found to present everyone's favorite backyard fare.

When it comes to the beef burger, the cut you choose is really important. And, despite what you might expect, this is one time when I generally prefer the cheaper option. On occasion I will make an "upscale" burger using the comparatively pricey ground sirloin, but for the most part, I go for inexpensive ground chuck. Look for beef that is marked 80 percent lean, 20 percent fat for the juiciest, tastiest burgers.

The same principal follows for ground poultry. Fat carries flavor and moisture, and without enough of it, your finished dish will be dry and lacking in taste. So while it is possible to find even 99-percent-lean ground white-meat turkey, look for some that includes dark meat in the mixture and has a percentage closer to 90 percent lean, 10 percent fat. Far more flavorful, it's still a remarkably healthy option. Poultry doesn't need to be looked at as just a healthy substitute for beef. That would be an injustice. It tastes great and, due to its mild flavor, it pairs with tons of spices and toppings to create really dynamic dishes.

For the truly health-conscious, buffalo is a fantastic option. It is naturally lean and is lower in fat and cholesterol than beef and even chicken! Ounce for ounce, it's also higher in iron and protein and is loaded with heart-healthy Omega-3 fatty acids. Buffalo is farm raised and has a nice, mild beef-like flavor that is never gamey. Because buffalo is so lean, you must be sure not to overcook it or else you run the risk of a dry burger. Available in some supermarkets and butcher shops, high-quality buffalo meat can also be easily found online.

Green Chile Cheeseburgers

I love a simple burger as much as the next person does, but I'm always willing to try to make a good thing great. And this is a great burger. I first tried one while in New Mexico and after my first bite, I knew I had to find a way to bring it to Mesa Grill. The green chile sauce is flavorful with a nice peppery—not hot—bite from the grilled poblanos. I add some heat at the end with pickled jalapeños. Delicious.

Serves 4

2 pounds ground chuck, 80 percent lean
2 tablespoons canola oil
Kosher salt and freshly ground black pepper
8 thin slices Chihuahua or provolone cheese

4 good-quality hamburger buns
Green Chile Sauce (recipe follows)
4 thick slices beefsteak tomatoes
4 pickled jalapeño chiles, thinly sliced

1. Heat your grill to high.

2. Form the meat into 4 burgers, each 1 inch thick. Brush with the oil and season liberally with salt and pepper on both sides. Place on the grill and grill until golden brown and slightly charred, 4 to 5 minutes. Turn the burgers over and continue cooking to medium, about 4 minutes longer.

3. Place 2 slices of the cheese on each burger, close the lid or tent with foil, and cook until the cheese has just melted, about 1 minute.

4. Place the burgers on the bun bottoms and top each one with a few tablespoons of the green chile sauce, a slice of tomato, and some pickled jalapeño. Place the bun tops on top and serve immediately.

Green Chile Sauce

Makes approximately ½ cup

2 poblano chiles, grilled (see page 120), peeled, seeded, and chopped
1 medium red onion, cut crosswise into ½-inch-thick slices, and grilled (see page 120)
2 cloves garlic, chopped

2 tablespoons chopped fresh cilantro or oregano leaves
1 tablespoon honey
¼ teaspoon kosher salt
¼ teaspoon freshly ground black pepper

Combine the poblanos, onion, garlic, cilantro, ¼ cup cold water, honey, salt, and pepper in a blender and blend until smooth. Adjust the salt and pepper. The sauce can be made 1 day in advance and kept covered in the refrigerator. Bring to room temperature before serving.

Texas Burger

I married a born and raised Texan who loves beef brisket with coleslaw and pickles. I love brisket, too, but making it is an all-day affair. So I created a burger that has all the same flavors but takes less than an hour to prepare. If you want to make it even faster, feel free to substitute your favorite store-bought barbecue sauce. Or my Mesa BBQ Sauce, available at www.BobbyFlay.com.

Serves 4

Coleslaw
¾ cup mayonnaise
½ small white onion, grated
2 tablespoons sugar
2 teaspoons celery seed
3 tablespoons apple-cider vinegar
Kosher salt and freshly ground black pepper
1 small head of cabbage, cored, finely shredded
1 large carrot, finely shredded

Burger
BBQ Sauce (recipe follows)
2 pounds ground chuck, 80 percent lean
2 tablespoons canola oil
Kosher salt and freshly ground black pepper
4 good-quality hamburger buns
Dill pickles, thinly sliced

1. To make the coleslaw, whisk together the mayonnaise, onion, sugar, celery seed, vinegar, and salt and pepper to taste in a large bowl. Add the cabbage and carrot and stir to combine. Season with additional salt and pepper, if needed. Cover and refrigerate for at least 15 minutes and up to 2 hours before serving.

2. Heat your grill to high. Divide the barbecue sauce between 2 bowls, one to use while grilling and one to use when the meat is cooked.

3. Form the meat into 4 burgers, each 1 inch thick. Brush with the oil and season liberally with salt and pepper on both sides. Place on the grill and grill until golden brown and slightly charred, 4 to 5 minutes. Brush with half of the barbecue sauce, turn the burgers over, and continue cooking to medium, about 4 minutes longer.

4. Place the burgers on the bun bottoms and spoon barbecue sauce over the burgers. Top with some of the coleslaw, a few pickles, and the bun tops and serve immediately.

(continued)

BBQ Sauce

Makes approximately 1¾ cups

2 tablespoons canola oil
1 large Spanish onion, coarsely chopped
4 cloves garlic, coarsely chopped
2 cups canned plum tomatoes and juices, pureed
¼ cup ketchup
¼ cup red wine vinegar
¼ cup Worcestershire sauce
3 tablespoons Dijon mustard

3 tablespoons dark brown sugar
2 tablespoons honey
¼ cup molasses
3 tablespoons ancho chile powder
3 tablespoons pasilla chile powder
2 to 4 canned chipotle chiles in adobo,
  pureed, to taste
Kosher salt and freshly ground black pepper

1. Heat the oil over medium-high heat in a heavy-bottomed medium saucepan. Add the onion and cook until soft, 3 to 4 minutes. Add the garlic and cook for 1 minute. Add the tomatoes and 1 cup water, bring to a boil, and simmer for 10 minutes. Add the ketchup, vinegar, Worcestershire, mustard, brown sugar, honey, molasses, both chile powders, and the chipotles and simmer, stirring occasionally, for an additional 30 to 40 minutes, until thickened.

2. Transfer the mixture to a food processor and puree until smooth. Season with salt and pepper to taste. Pour into a bowl and allow to cool to room temperature. The sauce will keep for 1 week in the refrigerator stored in a tightly sealed container.

Spicy Buffalo-Style Burger with Celery-Carrot Slaw and Blue Cheese Dressing

The "buffalo" in this burger is all in the preparation, not the meat, although you could use ground buffalo in this recipe. I love Buffalo chicken wings and have been known to polish off a platter with blue cheese dressing and a few beers in one sitting. So, I thought, why not take those flavorings and apply them to a burger? I have taken the celery and carrots that normally accompany the wings in stick form and turned them into a slaw with blue cheese dressing, which takes the place of the traditional blue cheese sauce. This could be one of my new favorites.

Serves 4

Carrot-Celery Slaw
¼ cup mayonnaise
¼ cup crumbled blue cheese
1 tablespoon fresh lemon juice
2 stalks celery, thinly sliced
2 medium carrots, shredded
2 tablespoons finely chopped fresh chives
Kosher salt and freshly ground black pepper

"Buffalo" Burgers
6 tablespoons unsalted butter
1 clove garlic, smashed
1 tablespoon ancho chile powder
¼ cup Bobby Flay's Mesa Grill Hot Sauce or your favorite hot sauce
Kosher salt
2 pounds ground chicken, turkey, or beef
2 tablespoons canola oil
Freshly ground black pepper
4 good-quality hamburger buns, split

1. To make the slaw, whisk together the mayonnaise, blue cheese, and lemon juice in a medium bowl. Add the celery, carrots, and chives and mix until combined. Season with salt and pepper. Cover and refrigerate for up to 1 hour.

2. Heat your grill to high.

3. Melt the butter over low heat in a small saucepan. Add the garlic, ancho powder, and hot sauce and cook until heated through, about 5 minutes. Season with salt. Let cool slightly and remove the garlic.

4. Form the meat into 4 burgers, each 1 inch thick. Brush with the oil and season liberally with salt and pepper. Grill the burgers, brushing every minute or so with the butter sauce, until golden brown on both sides and cooked completely through, about 5 minutes per side for chicken or turkey or, for beef, about 4 minutes per side for medium.

5. Place the burgers on the bottom half of each bun and top with some of the slaw and the bun tops. Serve immediately.

Blue Cheese Sirloin Burgers with Red Wine–Onion Jam

Beef, blue cheese, and red wine are a marriage of flavors made in heaven. This upscale burger is right off the pages of a steakhouse menu and will soon be a classic in your home. Buttering the roll and grilling it adds great flavor and texture; and no burger, in my opinon, is complete without a little strongly flavored mustard. I use Cabrales blue cheese from Spain, but Stilton from Great Britain, Roquefort from France, or Maytag blue from the good old USA will all work perfectly.

Serves 4

1½ pounds ground sirloin
2 tablespoons canola oil
Kosher salt and freshly ground black pepper
4 ounces blue cheese, cut into 4 slices
6 tablespoons unsalted butter, softened

4 hamburger buns or kaiser rolls, split
3 tablespoons Dijon mustard
1 cup watercress leaves
Red Wine–Onion Jam (recipe follows)

1. Heat your grill to high.

2. Shape the meat into 4 burgers, each 1 inch thick. Brush with oil and season liberally with salt and pepper on both sides. Place the burgers on the grill and grill until golden brown and slightly charred, 3 to 4 minutes. Turn the burgers over and continue grilling to medium, about 3 minutes longer. During the last minute of cooking, place a slice of cheese on top of each burger, close the cover of the grill, and allow the cheese to melt. Remove the burgers to a plate and let rest while you grill the buns.

3. Butter the cut sides of the buns and season with salt and pepper. Place on the grill, butter side down, and grill until lightly golden brown, about 30 seconds.

4. Spread some of the mustard on the bottom and top half of each bun and top with some of the watercress. Place the burgers on top of the watercress and spoon some of the onion jam on each burger. Top with the bun tops and serve immediately.

Red Wine–Onion Jam

Makes ¾ cup

2 tablespoons olive oil
2 medium red onions, halved and thinly sliced
1 cup dry red wine
2 tablespoons red wine vinegar

1 tablespoon honey
2 teaspoons finely chopped fresh thyme leaves
Kosher salt and freshly ground black pepper

Heat the oil in a medium sauté pan on the grates of the grill or on a stovetop over medium-low heat. Add the onion and cook until soft, stirring occasionally, about 10 minutes. Add the wine, vinegar, honey, and thyme and simmer, stirring occasionally, until the liquid has evaporated, 5 to 7 minutes. Season with salt and pepper. Remove from the heat and let cool to room temperature. The jam can be made 2 days in advance and stored in an airtight container in the refrigerator. Bring to room temperature before serving.

Nacho Burger

It seems only fitting that my love for southwestern ingredients would inspire me to create this burger. The mingling of creamy avocados and melted Monterey Jack cheese with spicy tomato salsa makes for one luscious flavor combination. I have replaced the usual lettuce with blue corn chips for crunch. See photograph on page 42.

Serves 4

2 pounds ground chuck, 80 percent lean
2 tablespoons canola oil
Kosher salt and freshly ground black pepper
8 (¼-inch-thick) slices Monterey Jack cheese
4 good-quality hamburger buns

Avocado Relish (recipe follows)
Tomato-Chipotle Salsa (recipe follows)
4 pickled jalapeño chiles, thinly sliced
½ cup coarsely crumbled blue corn tortilla
  chips

1. Heat your grill to high.

2. Form the meat into 4 burgers, each 1 inch thick. Brush with the oil and season liberally with salt and pepper on both sides. Place on the grill and grill until golden brown and slightly charred, 4 to 5 minutes. Turn the burgers over and continue cooking to medium, about 4 minutes longer.

3. Place 2 slices of the cheese on each burger, close the lid or tent with foil, and cook until the cheese has just melted, about 1 minute.

4. Remove the burgers from the grill and place on the bun bottoms. Top each burger with some of the avocado relish, some tomato-chipotle salsa, pickled jalapeños, and finally blue corn chips. Place the bun tops on top and serve immediately.

Avocado Relish

Makes approximately 1 cup

2 ripe Hass avocados, peeled, pitted, and
  coarsely chopped
3 tablespoons finely chopped red onion
1 jalapeño chile, finely chopped

Juice of 1 lime
2 tablespoons finely chopped fresh cilantro
  leaves
Kosher salt and freshly ground black pepper

Combine the avocados, onion, jalapeño, lime juice, cilantro, and salt and pepper to taste in a small bowl. The relish can be made 1 hour in advance and kept at room temperature.

Tomato-Chipotle Salsa

Makes approximately 1 cup

3 tablespoons red wine vinegar
2 teaspoons honey
1 tablespoon canola oil
2 teaspoons pureed canned chipotle chile in
  adobo

3 fresh plum tomatoes, seeded and finely
  diced
3 tablespoons finely chopped red onion
2 tablespoons finely chopped fresh cilantro
  leaves
Kosher salt

Stir together the vinegar, oil, honey, and chipotle puree in a medium bowl. Add the tomatoes, onion, and cilantro and mix to combine; season with salt. The salsa can be made 4 hours in advance and kept at room temperature.

Pressed Burger with Manchego, Serrano Ham, and Piquillo–Smoked Paprika Aioli

This burger is a lunchtime favorite at Bolo. Its premium Spanish ingredients make it entertainment worthy, but I'll warn you that it's hard to take your time and be polite while eating this scrumptious burger. The rich, smoky, and spicy-sweet aioli is just the beginning. Layering that with nutty manchego cheese and salty Serrano ham might be enough for a pretty good sandwich. But wrap that all around a juicy burger and press it into a crispy-on-the-outside, melted-on-the-inside, two-handed thing of wonder, and just try to hold yourself back.

Serves 4

1½ pounds ground chuck, 80 percent lean
3 tablespoons canola oil
Kosher salt and freshly ground black pepper
4 sesame seed hamburger buns

Piquillo–Smoked Paprika Aioli (recipe follows)
8 (¼-inch-thick) slices manchego cheese
8 paper-thin slices Serrano ham

1. Heat your grill to high.

2. Form the meat into 4 burgers, each 1 inch thick. Brush with 2 tablespoons of the oil and season liberally with salt and pepper on both sides. Place on the grill and grill until golden brown and slightly charred, 4 to 5 minutes. Turn the burgers over and continue cooking to medium-rare, about 3 minutes longer.

3. Place the bun bottoms on a flat surface and spread each one with a few table-spoons of the aioli. Top with a slice of cheese, then a slice of the ham, a burger, another slice of ham, and finally another slice of cheese.

4. Brush the sesame seed side of the bun tops with the remaining oil and place the entire sandwich on the grill, oiled side down. Using a heavy-duty metal spatula, press down on the bottom of the buns and grill until the tops are lightly golden brown, 1 to 2 minutes. Turn the burgers over and press down on the top and continue grilling until the bottom is lightly golden brown and the cheese has melted, about 1 minute longer. Serve immediately.

Piquillo–Smoked Paprika Aioli

Makes ¾ cup

½ cup mayonnaise
2 cloves garlic, chopped
2 piquillo peppers

2 teaspoons Spanish smoked paprika
½ teaspoon kosher salt

Combine the mayonnaise, garlic, peppers, paprika, and salt in a food processor and process until smooth. Cover and refrigerate for at least 30 minutes or up to 1 day before serving.

Buffalo Burger with Swiss Cheese, Red Cabbage Slaw, and Pickled Okra Russian Dressing

I serve buffalo occasionally at my restaurants. Buffalo is naturally low in fat and cholesterol and is a healthy alternative to beef. If it's not your thing, you can definitely use ground beef, turkey, or chicken in this recipe and it will be every bit as delicious. I like to think of this recipe as a cross between a burger and a Reuben sandwich.

Serves 4

Red Cabbage Slaw

¼ cup rice wine vinegar
2 teaspoons honey
2 tablespoons canola oil
Kosher salt and freshly ground black pepper
½ small head of red cabbage, finely shredded
1 large carrot, peeled and finely shredded

Burger

1½ pounds ground buffalo
2 tablespoons canola oil
Kosher salt and freshly ground black pepper
8 (¼-inch-thick) slices Gruyère or fontina cheese
Pickled Okra Russian Dressing (recipe follows)
4 good-quality hamburger buns

1. To make the slaw, whisk together the vinegar, honey, oil, and salt and pepper to taste in a large bowl. Add the cabbage and carrot and toss until combined. Let sit at room temperature for at least 15 minutes or up to 1 hour before serving.

2. Heat your grill to high.

3. Form the meat into 4 burgers, each 1 inch thick. Brush with the oil and season liberally with salt and pepper. Place on the grill and grill until golden brown and slightly charred, 3 to 4 minutes. Turn the burgers over and continue cooking to medium, about 3 minutes longer.

4. Place 2 slices of the cheese on each burger, close the lid or tent with foil, and cook until the cheese just begins to melt, about 1 minute.

5. Spread some of the Russian dressing on the tops and bottoms of each bun. Place a burger on each bottom half and top each burger with some of the slaw and a bun top. Serve immediately.

Pickled Okra Russian Dressing

Makes ¾ cup

½ cup mayonnaise
3 tablespoons ketchup
1 tablespoon Dijon mustard
3 tablespoons finely chopped red onion

¼ cup finely diced pickled okra
2 tablespoons finely chopped fresh flat-leaf parsley leaves
Kosher salt and freshly ground black pepper

Stir together the mayonnaise, ketchup, mustard, red onion, okra, and parsley in a medium bowl and season with salt and pepper. Cover and refrigerate for at least 30 minutes or up to 1 day before using.

Turkey Patty Melt with Grilled Onion Relish

Patty melts bring back fond memories of my childhood in the 1970s. I loved that perfectly cooked burger, topped with Swiss cheese and grilled onions, all crisped on the griddle until the rye bread was golden brown. I have updated the recipe by substituting turkey for beef (although you could definitely use beef). I've also tried to boost the flavor of both the onions and the cheese. Balsamic vinegar, Dijon mustard, and fresh thyme make this grilled-onion relish far more sophisticated than any plain sautéed onion, and I like Gruyère cheese as opposed to standard Swiss for its nuttier taste.

Serves 4

Relish
2 Spanish onions, cut crosswise into ½-inch-thick slices
2 tablespoons olive oil
Kosher salt and freshly ground black pepper
3 tablespoons balsamic vinegar
1 tablespoon Dijon mustard
1 tablespoon finely chopped fresh thyme leaves
¼ cup extra-virgin olive oil

Burgers
1½ pounds ground turkey, 90 percent lean
6 tablespoons olive oil
Kosher salt and freshly ground pepper
8 (¼-inch-thick) slices good-quality rye bread
8 (¼-inch-thick) slices Gruyère cheese
Dijon mustard, for serving
Ketchup, for serving

1. Heat your grill to high.

2. To make the relish, brush the onions on both sides with the 2 tablespoons olive oil and season with salt and pepper. Grill for 3 to 4 minutes on each side or until slightly charred and just cooked through. Transfer to a cutting board and coarsely chop.

3. Whisk together the vinegar, mustard, thyme, and salt and pepper to taste in a medium bowl. Whisk in the ¼ cup extra-virgin olive oil until emulsified. Add the onions and stir until combined. Let sit at room temperature while you cook the burgers.

4. Form the ground turkey into 4 burgers, each 1 inch thick. Brush with 2 tablespoons of the oil and season liberally with salt and pepper on both sides. Grill for 3 to 4 minutes per side for medium-well (the burger will continue to cook when placed back on the grill in the next step).

5. Place 4 slices of the bread on a flat surface and top each one with a slice of cheese and a few tablespoons of the grilled-onion relish. Put a burger, more relish, another slice of cheese, and the remaining 4 slices bread on top.

6. Brush the tops of the sandwiches with 2 tablespoons of the oil and place the sandwiches carefully on the grill, oiled side down. Press down slightly on the sandwiches with a metal spatula and grill for 1 to 2 minutes or until golden brown. Brush the top slices of bread with the remaining 2 tablespoons oil, flip over, press down with the spatula, and cook until that side is golden brown and the cheese has melted, 1 to 2 minutes.

7. Cut sandwiches in half and serve with mustard and ketchup on the side if desired.

Spiced Turkey Burgers
with Apple Raita and Spinach

A few years ago, for an ad campaign I was asked to create a turkey burger that consisted of turkey, Brie cheese, and grilled apples. It sounds like an odd combination, but the end result was really good. There was something about the mild flavor of turkey paired with the tart flavor of green apples that just worked. So when developing this take on the Middle Eastern classic meatball, kofte, I thought back to that turkey-apple flavor combination. Kofte is normally made with ground lamb and served with raita, a yogurt and cucumber sauce. While that tastes great, I like this lighter, bright-tasting version even better. It's also tasty served on grilled flatbread as a sandwich.

Serves 4

5 tablespoons olive oil
1 small red onion, finely grated
3 cloves garlic, finely chopped
3 tablespoons tomato paste
2 teaspoons ground cumin
1 teaspoon ground cinnamon
½ teaspoon ground allspice
¼ teaspoon cayenne pepper

Kosher salt and freshly ground black pepper
1½ pounds ground turkey, 90 percent lean
¼ cup finely chopped fresh flat-leaf parsley
  leaves
Juice of 1 lemon
2 tablespoons extra-virgin olive oil
8 ounces baby spinach
Apple Raita (recipe follows)

1. Heat 2 tablespoons of the oil in a medium sauté pan over medium-high heat. Add the onion and cook until slightly softened, about 2 minutes. Add the garlic and cook for 30 seconds. Add the tomato paste, 1 cup water, the cumin, cinnamon, allspice, and cayenne and season with salt and pepper. Cook until the mixture is thickened, about 2 minutes. Transfer to a large bowl and let cool slightly.

2. Add the turkey and parsley to the onion mixture and, using your hands, gently mix until combined. Cover the mixture and refrigerate for at least 1 hour or up to 8 hours to allow the flavors to meld.

3. Heat your grill to high.

4. Divide the mixture into 12 equal portions and roll into balls. Gently press down on the top of each patty to flatten slightly. Brush the patties on both sides with the remaining 3 tablespoons olive oil and season with salt and pepper.

5. Grill the burgers until golden brown on both sides and cooked through, about 3 minutes per side.

6. Whisk together the lemon juice and extra-virgin olive oil in a large bowl and season with salt and pepper. Add the spinach and toss to lightly coat the leaves in the dressing. Transfer the spinach to a platter and arrange the burgers on top of the leaves. Top each patty with some of the raita.

Apple Raita
Makes 1¾ cups

1 cup Greek yogurt
1 Granny Smith apple, cored and finely diced,
  plus more for garnish (optional)

½ teaspoon kosher salt
Pinch of ground cinnamon
Pinch of cayenne pepper

Stir together the yogurt, apple, salt, cinnamon, and cayenne in a small bowl. Cover and refrigerate for at least 30 minutes or up to 2 hours to allow the flavors to meld. Garnish with apple before serving, if desired.

chicken

Perfectly Grilled Chicken Breasts • Individual Grilled Chicken "Muffuletta" Sandwiches with Spicy Olive Relish • Grilled Chicken with Roasted Garlic–Oregano Vinaigrette and Grilled Fingerling Potatoes • Apple-Ginger Glazed Chicken • Sixteen-Spice–Rubbed Chicken Breast with Black Pepper Vinegar Sauce and Green Onion Slaw • Grilled Chicken Breasts with Tangerine-Maple–Black Pepper Glaze • Grilled Chicken Thighs with Green Olives and Sherry Vinegar–Orange Sauce • Spanish Spice–Rubbed Chicken Breasts with Parsley-Mint Sauce • Sweet-and-Sour Grilled Chicken • Chipotle-Honey–Glazed Chicken Wings with Toasted Sesame Seeds and Green Onion

We love chicken. It's high in protein, low in fat, inexpensive, and adaptable to a myriad of flavors and preparations. Chicken legs, wings, thighs, breasts . . . you can do so much with this bird that you could feed it to your family for weeks on end without anyone getting bored.

I can't imagine that there are many people out there who could find fault with a juicy grilled chicken breast. (A dry, charred-on-the-outside, raw-in-the-middle one maybe, but in this chapter I'll give you the tips to ensure that never happens to you again.) The great thing about chicken is how many different ways you can season and flavor it. Chicken is a global kitchen staple and is therefore a perfect match with most ethnic cuisines imaginable.

While I would guess that most people prefer (or at least think that they do) white breast meat, there are so many other options to consider. Grilled chicken thighs are a personal favorite. The meat is tender, juicy, and flavorful. Their popularity is on the rise and you can find them in your supermarket aisles both bone-in and skin-on and boneless and skinless. Pound for pound, thighs are also less expensive than breasts. Regardless of the cut, I generally prefer to cook my poultry on the bone as it makes for a juicier end result.

When it comes to shopping for chicken, I look for one of two kinds: either kosher or free-range. These may be a bit pricier than your standard brands, but what you get in return—a more flavorful, juicier, and better-tasting bird—is worth the extra cost. You should be able to find one or the other, if not both, at most major supermarkets. There are also great shopping resources available on the Web (see Sources, page 277).

Perfectly Grilled Chicken Breasts

I would say that one of the most frequent cooking questions I am asked is, "What's the secret to cooking moist chicken?" And though it may sound flip, my answer is always: don't overcook it. It's really that simple. While it is true, for safety reasons, that chicken must be cooked all the way through, that doesn't mean that it has to look and taste like leather. Boneless chicken breasts take fewer than 10 minutes to cook and need to rest for about 5 minutes before slicing, to allow the juices to recirculate through the meat.

It will also help if you pound the chicken to an even thickness so that it cooks evenly and keep the skin on to add extra moistness while cooking. If you are watching your weight or don't want to eat the skin, just remove it after you cook the chicken. Finally, make sure the grill is good and hot. Since the breast will cook quickly, you want to make sure you get a good crust on the outside before the inside is cooked.

When you buy boneless chicken breasts they have a tapered shape and a tenderloin attached. For grilling purposes it is best to remove the tenderloin, since its thin shape will cook much too fast to be any good before the rest of the chicken is cooked. Grill the tenderloins together for about two minutes per side until just cooked through.

Serves 4

4 (8-ounce) boneless chicken breasts
2 tablespoons canola oil

Kosher salt and freshly ground black pepper

1. Heat your grill to high.

2. Place the chicken between 2 pieces of plastic wrap and, using a meat mallet or the bottom of a heavy sauté pan, pound the chicken lightly to an even ½-inch thickness.

3. Brush the breasts on both sides with the oil and season with salt and pepper. Place the breasts on the grill, skin side down, and cook until golden brown and slightly charred, 4 to 5 minutes. Flip the chicken over and continue grilling until just cooked through, 3 to 4 minutes longer. An instant-read thermometer inserted into the center should register 155 degrees F.

4. Remove from the grill, tent with foil, and let rest for 5 minutes before serving.

Individual Grilled Chicken "Muffuletta" Sandwiches with Spicy Olive Relish

It's not exactly like the muffuletta that you will find at Central Grocery (where the sandwich originated in 1906) in New Orleans, but I incorporated two of the key ingredients—olive relish and provolone cheese—to make my own grilled chicken version. Muffulettas are always served cold, and you could assemble the sandwiches and then weight them down in the refrigerator if you're a big fan of the original; but I like to serve these hot, so the bread is crisp and the cheese oozes.

Serves 4

Spicy Olive Relish
2 small red bell peppers, grilled (see page 120), peeled, seeded, and diced
2 small yellow bell peppers, grilled (see page 120), peeled, seeded, and diced
1 serrano chile, grilled (see page 120) and finely diced
1 small red onion, cut into ½-inch-thick slices, grilled (see page 120) and coarsely chopped
3 cloves garlic, finely chopped
½ cup green olives, pitted and coarsely chopped
1 large stalk celery, finely diced
2 tablespoons capers, drained

¼ cup red wine vinegar
¼ cup extra-virgin olive oil
3 tablespoons coarsely chopped fresh flat-leaf parsley leaves
1 tablespoon finely chopped fresh oregano leaves
Kosher salt and freshly ground black pepper

Muffuletta
4 soft hero rolls
8 (¼-inch-thick) slices provolone cheese
Perfectly Grilled Chicken Breasts (page 65), sliced ¼ inch-thick

1. To make the spicy olive relish, combine the red and yellow peppers, the serrano, onion, garlic, olives, celery, capers, vinegar, oil, parsley, and oregano in a medium bowl and season with salt and pepper. Let sit at room temperature for at least 30 minutes before serving or keep covered for up to 1 day in the refrigerator. Bring to room temperature before serving.

2. Heat your grill to high.

3. Slice each roll three-quarters of the way through lengthwise. Place 1 slice of cheese on the bottom half of each roll and top with some of the olive relish, sliced chicken, more relish, and then another piece of cheese. Tightly close the sandwiches and wrap each sandwich in a sheet of aluminum foil.

4. Place 2 sandwiches, top side down, side by side on the grill and place a brick on top. Repeat with the remaining 2 sandwiches. Grill for 2 minutes. Remove the bricks, turn the sandwiches over, replace the bricks, and continue grilling for 2 to 3 minutes longer or until the cheese has melted.

Grilled Chicken with Roasted Garlic–Oregano Vinaigrette and Grilled Fingerling Potatoes

This recipe is a take on an Italian American dish called Chicken Vesuvio, which, to the best of my knowledge, can be found only in Chicago. The origins of the dish are unknown, but it has been suggested that it was first made popular by the Chicago restaurant Vesuvio in the 1930s. The original recipe is made with a cut-up whole chicken combined with lots of olive oil, white wine, oregano, red chile flakes, and garlic and then roasted with potatoes and peas in the oven until golden brown. My recipe utilizes the same flavors and ingredients but is adapted for the grill.

Serves 4

12 fingerling potatoes, scrubbed
Kosher salt
4 (8-ounce) bone-in chicken breasts
6 tablespoons olive oil

Freshly ground black pepper
Roasted Garlic–Oregano Vinaigrette (recipe follows)
Fresh oregano sprigs, for garnish

1. Put the potatoes in a medium saucepan, cover with salted cold water, and bring to a boil. Reduce the heat and simmer until a paring knife inserted into the potatoes comes out with some resistance, 8 to 10 minutes. Do not cook the potatoes all the way through because they will continue cooking on the grill. Drain well, and when cool enough to handle, slice in half lengthwise.

2. Heat your grill to medium.

3. Brush the chicken and potatoes with the oil and season with salt and pepper. Place the chicken on the grill, skin side down, and grill until golden brown and slightly charred, 6 to 7 minutes. Turn the chicken over and continue grilling until just cooked through, 5 to 6 minutes. A few minutes before the chicken has finished cooking, place the potatoes on the grill, cut side down, and cook until lightly golden brown, about 2 minutes. Turn over and continue grilling about a minute longer.

4. Remove the chicken and potatoes to a platter and immediately drizzle with the roasted garlic–oregano vinaigrette. Tent with foil and let rest for 5 minutes before serving. Garnish with oregano sprigs.

Roasted Garlic–Oregano Vinaigrette

Makes approximately 1 cup

8 cloves roasted garlic (page 38)
¼ cup white wine vinegar
1 teaspoon honey
2 tablespoons fresh oregano leaves

½ teaspoon kosher salt
¼ teaspoon red chile flakes
¾ cup extra-virgin olive oil

Combine the garlic, vinegar, honey, oregano, salt, and chile flakes in a blender and blend until smooth. With the motor running, slowly add the oil and process until emulsified. The vinaigrette can be made 1 day in advance, covered, and refrigerated. Bring to room temperature before serving.

Apple-Ginger–Glazed Chicken

This apple-ginger glaze is an extremely easy way to transform boring chicken breasts into a delectable dinner. There's a good chance you have many of these ingredients somewhere in your kitchen already! Apple jelly is mild, melts into a glaze beautifully, and is a great base to carry the slightly spicy flavor of fresh ginger onto the chicken. This is one of my lighter glazes and will make everyone in your family happy.

Serves 4

½ cup apple jelly
2 tablespoons low-sodium soy sauce
1 tablespoon finely chopped fresh thyme
1 tablespoon grated peeled fresh ginger

¼ teaspoon fresh ground black pepper
Perfectly Grilled Chicken Breasts
    (page 65)

1. Heat your grill to medium-high.

2. Whisk together the jelly, soy sauce, thyme, ginger, and pepper in a small saucepan and bring to a simmer on the grates of the grill. Cook for 3 minutes, stirring constantly, then remove from the grill, and let cool slightly.

3. Brush the glaze on the chicken breasts during their last 2 minutes of grilling. Remove the chicken to a platter and brush with the remaining glaze. Tent with foil and let rest for 5 minutes before serving.

Sixteen Spice–Rubbed Chicken Breast with Black Pepper Vinegar Sauce and Green Onion Slaw

I developed this sixteen-spice rub at Mesa Grill years ago and I've been using it on chicken in some way or other ever since. It's complex, slightly sweet and spicy, and well-rounded in taste—plus, it makes for a really nice crusty exterior. (If you don't feel like investing in all of the spices, you can actually buy it already prepared on my Web site, www.bobbyflay.com.) The black pepper vinegar sauce has a clean flavor with just the right combination of acidic, spicy, and sweet elements. Green onion slaw is gorgeous—bright purple flecked with green, fresh and crunchy. It's great with this chicken but I think you'll find it becoming a grilling staple in your house.

Serves 4

Green Onion Slaw
1 cup coarsely chopped green onions,
    white and green parts
¼ cup red wine vinegar
2 teaspoons honey
2 serrano chiles
2 tablespoons mayonnaise
½ cup canola oil
Kosher salt and freshly ground black pepper
1 small head of purple cabbage, finely shredded
1 small red onion, halved and thinly sliced
2 teaspoons poppy seeds
¼ cup chopped fresh cilantro leaves

Chicken
1 tablespoon ancho chile powder
1 tablespoon pasilla chile powder
1 tablespoon ground cumin
1 tablespoon ground coriander
1 tablespoon ground ginger
1 tablespoon brown sugar
2 teaspoons garlic powder
2 teaspoons onion powder
1 teaspoon ground allspice
1 teaspoon ground cinnamon
1 teaspoon ground cloves
1 teaspoon ground fennel seeds
Heaping ¼ teaspoon chile de árbol
Kosher salt
2 teaspoons coarsely ground black pepper
Heaping ¼ teaspoon cayenne pepper
4 (8-ounce) boneless chicken breasts, skin on
¼ cup canola oil
Black Pepper Vinegar Sauce (recipe follows)

1. To make the dressing for the slaw, combine the green onions, vinegar, honey, chiles, mayonnaise, oil, and salt and pepper to taste in a blender and blend until emulsified.

2. Combine the cabbage, red onion, and poppy seeds in a bowl, add the dressing, and stir until combined. Fold in the cilantro and season with salt and pepper to taste. Cover and refrigerate while you grill the chicken or for up to 1 hour.

(continued)

3. Heat your grill to high.

4. Stir together the ancho powder, pasilla powder, cumin, coriander, ginger, brown sugar, garlic powder, onion powder, allspice, cinnamon, cloves, fennel, chile de árbol, 2 tablespoons salt, black pepper, and cayenne in a small bowl.

5. Brush both sides of the breasts with the oil and season with salt. Rub the top side of each breast with a few tablespoons of the rub and place on the grill, rub side down. Grill until golden brown and slightly charred, 3 to 4 minutes. Turn the breasts over and continue grilling until just cooked through, 4 to 5 minutes longer.

6. Remove the chicken from the grill and drizzle with the black pepper vinegar sauce. Tent loosely with foil and let rest for 5 minutes. Serve the slaw on the side.

Black Pepper Vinegar Sauce
Makes ¾ cup

¼ cup rice wine vinegar
½ cup extra-virgin olive oil
3 tablespoons Dijon mustard

2 teaspoons honey
1 teaspoon kosher salt
¾ teaspoon coarsely ground black pepper

Combine the vinegar, oil, mustard, honey, salt, and pepper in a blender and blend until smooth. The sauce can be made 1 day in advance, covered, and refrigerated. Bring to room temperature before serving.

Grilled Chicken Breasts with Tangerine-Maple-Black Pepper Glaze

You could use plain orange juice and orange zest here, but do try to find tangerines. They are just a bit more acidic, and I think that slightly sour note is crucial to creating a successful balance with the sweet maple syrup and spicy black pepper. The soy sauce may seem to be out of left field, but its earthiness makes for a much more rounded taste than would salt, and its deep color is a nice bonus in the glaze.

Serves 4

1 tablespoon canola oil
1 small red onion, coarsely chopped
Grated zest of 1 tangerine or orange
1 quart tangerine juice or tangerine-orange juice
  (not from concentrate)
4 fresh thyme sprigs
¼ cup pure maple syrup

1 tablespoon low-sodium soy sauce
1 teaspoon coarsely ground black pepper
Perfectly Grilled Chicken Breasts (page 65)
2 green onions, white and green parts,
  thinly sliced

1. Heat the oil in a medium saucepan over high heat, add the onion, and cook until soft, 3 to 4 minutes. Add the zest, juice, and thyme; bring to a boil; and cook, stirring occasionally, until thickened and reduced to approximately ½ cup, 20 to 25 minutes.

2. Strain the mixture into a bowl and whisk in the syrup, soy sauce, and pepper. Let cool to room temperature. The glaze can be made 2 days in advance, covered, and refrigerated. Bring to room temperature before using.

3. Brush the glaze on the chicken breasts during the last minute of grilling. Remove from the grill, place on a platter, and brush with more of the glaze. Tent loosely with foil and let rest for 5 minutes. Garnish with the green onions before serving.

Grilled Chicken Thighs with Green Olives and Sherry Vinegar–Orange Sauce

Unlike breast meat, chicken thighs seem to stay moist no matter how long you cook them. The dark, dense meat is able to stand up to assertive flavors such as the vinegar and rosemary in this sauce. Chicken thighs are not only extra flavorful, they also have a sturdy texture that makes them perfect for grilling. Grilled oranges (see page 192) would make a nice garnish here; squeeze them over the chicken for an extra bit of orange.

Serves 4

4 tablespoons olive oil
2 shallots, coarsely chopped
1 clove garlic, coarsely chopped
Grated zest of 1 orange
2 cups orange juice (not from concentrate)
3 tablespoons aged sherry vinegar

1 cup low-sodium chicken broth
2 fresh rosemary sprigs, plus extra for garnish
3 tablespoons honey
Kosher salt and freshly ground black pepper
4 (8-ounce) bone-in chicken thighs
½ cup picholine olives, pitted

1. Heat 2 tablespoons of the oil in a medium saucepan over high heat. Add the shallots and cook until soft and lightly golden brown, 2 to 3 minutes. Add the garlic and cook for 30 seconds. Add the orange zest and juice and the vinegar and bring to a boil. Cook, stirring occasionally, until reduced by half, 5 to 7 minutes. Add the broth and rosemary and simmer until reduced by half and slightly thickened, 8 to 10 minutes.

2. Strain the sauce into a bowl, stir in the honey, and season with salt and pepper. The sauce can be made 1 day in advance, covered, and refrigerated. Reheat before using.

3. Heat your grill to medium.

4. Brush the chicken on both sides with the remaining 2 tablespoons oil and season with salt and pepper. Place the chicken on the grill, skin side down, and cook until golden brown and slightly charred, 4 to 5 minutes. Turn the thighs over, close the cover of the grill, and continue cooking until just cooked through, 6 to 7 minutes longer.

5. Remove the thighs to a platter and drizzle with some of the sauce. Tent loosely with foil and let rest for 5 minutes. Scatter the olives around the platter and garnish with rosemary sprigs. Serve additional sauce on the side.

Spanish Spice–Rubbed Chicken Breasts with Parsley-Mint Sauce

Another Bolo dish, this chicken is flavored with the same spice rub that I use on our steak there. It's a versatile rub and is also great with pork and, of course, turkey. The joys of rubs such as this—especially when applied to chicken—are two-fold. Not only does the mild flavor of the meat get a great boost of flavor, the rub also creates a crust, adding another layer of texture. The fresh and herbaceous parsley-mint sauce gets a nice kick from garlic and serrano chiles, and its splash of bright green is a wonderful counterpoint to the mahogany-colored chicken. See photograph on page 62.

Serves 4

2 tablespoons Spanish paprika
1½ teaspoons ground cumin
1½ teaspoons dry mustard
1½ teaspoons ground fennel seed
1 teaspoon coarsely ground black pepper

2 teaspoons kosher salt
4 (8-ounce) bone-in chicken breasts
¼ cup olive oil
Parsley-Mint Sauce (recipe follows)
Fresh mint sprigs, for garnish (optional)

1. Heat your grill to high.

2. Whisk together the paprika, cumin, mustard, fennel, pepper, and salt in a small bowl.

3. Brush the chicken with the oil on both sides. Rub the breasts on the skin side with some of the rub and place on the grill, rub side down. Grill until golden brown and slightly charred, 4 to 5 minutes. Turn the breasts over and continue cooking until just cooked through, 4 to 5 minutes.

4. Transfer the chicken to a platter and immediately drizzle with some of the parsley-mint sauce. Tent loosely with foil and let rest for 5 minutes. Serve with additional sauce on the side and garnish with mint, if desired.

Parsley-Mint Sauce

Makes approximately 1 cup

1½ cups tightly packed fresh flat-leaf parsley
   leaves
¾ cup tightly packed fresh mint leaves
3 cloves garlic, chopped
2 serrano chiles, grilled (see page 120), peeled,
   and chopped

2 tablespoons honey
2 tablespoons Dijon mustard
¾ cup olive oil
Kosher salt and freshly ground black pepper

1. Combine the parsley, mint, garlic, and serranos in a food processor and process
   until coarsely chopped. Add the honey and mustard and process until combined.
   With the motor running, slowly add the olive oil and blend until emulsified.

2. Transfer the mixture to a bowl and whisk in a few tablespoons cold water to thin to
   a sauce-like consistency. Season with salt and pepper to taste. The sauce can be
   made 8 hours in advance and stored, covered, in the refrigerator. Bring to room
   temperature before serving.

Sweet-and-Sour Grilled Chicken

Okay, so it's not the same chicken that comes from your neighborhood Chinese
restaurant. But I have to tell you, it has every bit as much flavor as the original with
the added benefit of being much healthier since the chicken is grilled, not breaded
and deep-fried. And because I love heat, I threw in a jalapeño for good measure.

Serves 4

1 cup red wine vinegar
½ cup distilled white vinegar
1 cup pineapple juice
1 cup sugar
1 jalapeño chile, coarsely chopped
1 (2-inch) piece fresh ginger, peeled and
   chopped

½ large red bell pepper, finely diced
½ large yellow bell pepper, finely diced
3 tablespoons finely chopped fresh cilantro
   leaves, plus more for garnish
Kosher salt
Perfectly Grilled Chicken Breasts
   (page 65)

1. Combine both vinegars, the pineapple juice, sugar, jalapeño, and ginger in a
   medium saucepan and simmer over medium heat, stirring occasionally, until
   reduced by half, 12 to 15 minutes. Strain the sauce into a bowl, stir in the red
   and yellow pepper and cilantro, and season with salt.

2. Remove the chicken from the grill and immediately drizzle with the sauce. Tent
   loosely with foil and let rest for 5 minutes. Garnish with cilantro before serving.

Chipotle-Honey-Glazed Chicken Wings with Toasted Sesame Seeds and Green Onion

Even though this version of hot wings is healthier than the classic—which is deep-fried and tossed in lots of butter and hot sauce—it's every bit as tasty.

Serves 4 to 6

1 cup honey
2 to 3 tablespoons pureed canned chipotle chiles
   in adobo
2 tablespoons Dijon mustard
4 tablespoons ancho chile powder
Kosher salt and freshly ground black pepper
4 tablespoons canola oil
2 teaspoons ground coriander

2 teaspoons ground cumin
2 teaspoons Spanish paprika
3 pounds chicken wings
2 tablespoons sesame seeds, toasted
   (see page 19)
3 green onions, white and green parts,
   thinly sliced

1. Heat your grill to medium-high

2. Whisk together the honey, chipotle puree, 1 tablespoon of the mustard, 1 tablespoon of the ancho powder, 1 teaspoon salt, and 2 tablespoons of the oil in a small bowl. Divide the glaze evenly between 2 bowls, one small, the other large.

3. Stir together the remaining 3 tablespoons of ancho powder with the coriander, cumin, and paprika in a small bowl.

4. Rinse the chicken wings under cold water and pat dry with paper towels. Cut the tips off the wings and discard (or freeze and use for making chicken stock). Cut each wing into 2 pieces through the joint.

5. Place the chicken wings in a large bowl, add the spice rub and the remaining 2 tablespoons oil, and toss to coat. Season with salt and pepper and place the wings on the grill in an even layer. Grill until golden brown and slightly charred, 4 to 5 minutes. Reduce the heat of the grill to medium, turn the wings over, and close the lid of the grill. Continue grilling until just cooked through, 15 to 20 minutes longer, brushing with the small bowl of glaze every few minutes and turning once during the last 10 minutes of cooking.

6. Transfer the wings to the large bowl, brush with the reserved glaze, and toss to coat. Transfer to a platter and sprinkle with the sesame seeds and green onions.

corn

One of summer's greatest joys is the local farm-fresh produce that fills markets and roadside stands. There are juicy tomatoes, ruby strawberries, snappy green beans, and just-picked ears of sweet corn. Most of these things you might be able to find year-round, imported from somewhere or another. Much of it is even pretty good stuff these days. But when it comes to corn, I'm a summer-only guy. Fresh corn is so sweet and so tender that once you've had it, nothing else will really do.

Sweet corn is an extremely delicate crop and needs to be prepared as soon after it is picked as possible. The sugar in the kernels begins its conversion into starch the moment the ear is harvested. Most sweet corn out there these days is some sort of hybrid developed with the aim of slowing that conversion of sugar to starch, buying the grower a day or two to get you a sweet, high-quality ear of corn. But I wouldn't want to push it more than that, and for that reason I buy and recommend that others buy only the freshest corn out there when it's in season—no frozen ears or winter imports for me.

In your search for the freshest ear, try to find a market that gets its corn from local growers and has a high product turnover. When picking corn, peel back the husks and inspect the kernels. The kernels should appear rounded, individual, and pearly. Flattened and compacted rows indicate a starchy, overgrown ear. The husks should hug the ear tightly and be bright and green. Another thing to look for is dry, not soggy, silks.

A steamed ear of corn, dripping with butter, may be the way most people envision this summer treat, but I think that a perfectly grilled ear of corn is the way to go. Leaving a layer of husk on keeps the corn nice and juicy, while the fire of the grill infuses it with smokiness and gives the kernels a toasty caramelization that can't be beat.

Perfectly Grilled Corn

Each year I wait for the end of summer so I can eat fresh Jersey corn on the cob until I burst. When I was growing up, my mom, like every mom at that time, would husk the corn and boil it in salted water. While I have fond memories of corn prepared that way, once I became a chef, I learned that grilling or roasting corn in its husks is a far superior way to prepare it. Boiling corn in water seems to leach out the flavor. It's also all too easy to overcook corn this way, giving the kernels a mushy consistency. Grilling it in the husks steams it and concentrates the natural sweet flavor while imparting the taste of the husk into the corn. Corn prepared this way is so good that all it needs is some butter and salt. However, I have included more than half a dozen other ways to use it in this chapter that are every bit as good.

Serves 4

8 ears corn | Kosher salt

1. Heat your grill to medium.

2. Pull the outer husks down each ear to the stalk end. Strip away the silk from each ear of corn by hand. Fold the husks back into place and tie the ends together with kitchen string. Place the ears of corn in a large bowl of cold water with 1 tablespoon of salt for 10 minutes.

3. Remove the corn from the water and shake off the excess. Place the corn on the grill, close the cover, and grill for 15 to 20 minutes, turning every 5 minutes, or until the kernels are tender when pierced with a paring knife.

4. Remove the husks from the cobs before eating the corn.

To remove corn kernels from the cob
Stand the cob upright on its stalk end in a large bowl or pan. Hold the tip with your fingers and cut down the sides of the cob with a sharp paring knife, releasing the kernels without cutting into the cob. Run the dull edge of the knife down the naked cob to release any remaining corn and liquid.

Grilled Corn and Tomato Cracked Wheat Salad

You won't find corn, balsamic vinegar, and basil in the tabbouleh at Middle Eastern restaurants. The classic version is made with bulgur wheat combined with lots of mint and parsley, tomatoes, and lemon juice. But the bulgur wheat provides a blank canvas for any ingredient you want to use, and I love the combination of flavors in this great summer side dish.

Serves 4

Kosher salt
1 cup bulgur wheat
4 ears Perfectly Grilled Corn (page 83)
3 tablespoons canola oil
Freshly ground black pepper
¼ cup finely chopped fresh flat-leaf parsley leaves
¼ cup finely chopped fresh chives

¼ cup finely chopped fresh basil leaves
2 ripe beefsteak or 4 plum tomatoes, halved, seeded, and finely diced
1 small red onion, finely diced
3 tablespoons balsamic vinegar
2 tablespoons fresh lemon juice
1 clove garlic, finely chopped
½ cup extra-virgin olive oil

1. Bring 3 cups of water to a boil in a medium saucepan. Add 1 tablespoon of salt and stir in the bulgur wheat. Cover the pot, turn off the heat, and let sit for 30 minutes or until the bulgur is tender. Drain well and press out any excess water. Place in a large bowl.

2. Heat your grill to high.

3. Remove the husks from the grilled corn and discard. Brush the ears of corn with the canola oil and season with salt and pepper. Grill the ears until the kernels are lightly golden brown on all sides, about 5 minutes.

4. Remove the kernels from the cobs (see page 83) and place the kernels in the bowl with the bulgur. Add the parsley, chives, basil, tomatoes, and onion and toss to combine.

5. Whisk together the vinegar, lemon juice, garlic, and extra-virgin olive oil in a small bowl and season with salt and pepper. Pour the mixture over the bulgur mixture and stir well to combine. Let sit at room temperature for at least 30 minutes before serving. The tabbouleh can be made 1 day in advance and stored, covered, in the refrigerator. Serve cold or at room temperature.

Charred Corn Guacamole with Corn Chips

I love the smoky flavor and crunch that grilled corn gives to the buttery flavor and texture of avocado. This guacamole also goes well atop grilled fish and chicken. The corn in this recipe is actually grilled twice—once to cook it through and secondly to get a nice char on the outside to add extra smoky flavor and great texture to the guacamole. See photograph on page 80.

Serves 4

4 ears Perfectly Grilled Corn (page 83)
4 tablespoons canola oil
Kosher salt and freshly ground black pepper
3 ripe Hass avocados, peeled, pitted, and diced
1 serrano chile, finely diced

1 small red onion, finely diced
Juice of 1 lime
¼ cup chopped fresh cilantro leaves
Blue, yellow, and white corn chips, for serving

1. Heat your grill to high.

2. Brush the ears of grilled corn with 2 tablespoons of the oil and season with salt and pepper. Grill the ears until they are lightly golden brown on all sides, about 5 minutes. Remove the kernels from the cobs (see page 83).

3. Place the avocados in a medium bowl and mash slightly with a fork. Add the corn kernels, serrano, onion, lime juice, cilantro, the remaining 2 tablespoons oil, and salt and pepper to taste and gently stir to combine. Serve with corn chips for dipping.

Grilled Corn and Tomato–Sweet Onion Salad with Fresh Basil Dressing and Crumbled Blue Cheese

This salad is (or should be, at least) a summer classic. It is a celebration of those wonderful ingredients—summer corn and ripe tomatoes—that grace markets for only a short time every year. The dressing is a favorite of mine, sweet and fresh and summery. (I also like to drizzle it in place of the standard olive oil and whole basil leaves in a fresh mozzarella and tomato salad for a slightly different take on the classic caprese salad.) Sharp and tangy blue cheese provides just the right salty touch to balance out the otherwise sweet nature of the salad.

Serves 4

¼ cup rice wine vinegar
¼ cup chopped fresh basil leaves
2 teaspoons honey
Kosher salt and freshly ground black pepper
½ cup extra-virgin olive oil
Perfectly Grilled Corn (page 83), kernels removed from the cobs

2 sweet onions (such as Vidalia or Walla Walla), halved and thinly sliced
1 pint Sweet 100, grape, or cherry tomatoes, halved
8 ounces blue cheese, crumbled
Fresh basil sprigs, for serving

1. Combine the vinegar, chopped basil, honey, 1 teaspoon salt, ¼ teaspoon pepper, and the oil in a blender and blend until smooth. The dressing can be made 2 hours in advance and refrigerated. Bring to room temperature before using.

2. Combine the corn kernels, onion, and tomatoes in a large bowl. Add the dressing and toss to coat; season with salt and pepper. Let sit at room temperature for 30 minutes before serving. The salad can be made 1 day in advance and stored, covered, in the refrigerator.

3. Top with crumbled blue cheese and garnish with basil sprigs before serving cold or at room temperature.

Charred Corn and Grilled Shrimp Chopped Salad with Tortilla Chips and Lime Dressing

I love chopped salads almost as much as I love coming up with new and interesting combinations to put in them. This particular version is inspired by southwestern ingredients, which I obviously love, and is all about flavor and texture: smokiness from the charred corn and shrimp, spiciness from the pickled jalapeños, tartness from the dressing, and crunchiness from the tortilla chips. This salad is perfect as a starter to any meal and filling enough to be served as the main course.

Serves 4

6 ears Perfectly Grilled Corn (page 83)
¼ cup canola oil
Kosher salt and freshly ground black pepper
12 ounces large (21 to 24 count) shrimp, peeled, deveined, and cooked as for Perfectly Grilled Shrimp (page 219)
4 pickled jalapeños, drained and thinly sliced
1 large ripe Hass avocado, peeled, pitted, and finely diced

2 ripe beefsteak tomatoes, seeded and finely diced
3 tablespoons fresh lime juice
1 tablespoon rice wine vinegar
2 teaspoons honey
½ cup extra-virgin olive oil
¼ cup fresh cilantro leaves
2 cups coarsely chopped watercress or romaine lettuce
½ cup coarsely crushed tortilla chips

1. Heat your grill to high.

2. Brush the grilled ears of corn with the canola oil and season with salt and pepper. Grill until slightly charred on all sides, about 4 minutes. Remove the cobs from the grill and let cool slightly. Remove the kernels from the cobs and transfer to a medium bowl.

3. Cut the shrimp in half and add to the corn kernels along with the jalapeños, avocado, and tomatoes.

4. Whisk together the lime juice, vinegar, honey, and extra-virgin olive oil in a small bowl and season with salt and pepper. Pour the dressing over the corn salad, add the cilantro leaves, and toss to combine. Season with salt and pepper. The corn salad can be made up to 1 hour in advance, covered, and refrigerated.

5. Arrange the watercress on a large platter and spoon the corn salad over the top. Sprinkle with the tortilla chips.

Grilled Corn with Toasted Garlic-Thyme Butter

Toasting garlic gives it a slightly nutty flavor that mirrors the nutty flavor of the charred corn. The delicate lemony flavor of thyme cuts through the richness of the butter, adding a freshness and almost citrus-like flavor.

Serves 4

2 tablespoons canola oil
3 cloves garlic, coarsely chopped
2 tablespoons fresh thyme leaves
12 tablespoons (1½ sticks) unsalted butter, slightly softened

Kosher salt and freshly ground black pepper
Perfectly Grilled Corn (page 83)

1. Heat the oil in a small sauté pan over medium heat. Add the garlic and cook until lightly golden brown, 3 to 4 minutes. Remove from the heat and stir in the thyme leaves. Let cool slightly.

2. Combine the butter and the garlic mixture in a food processor and process until smooth. Season with salt and pepper. Cover and refrigerate for at least 30 minutes or up to 4 hours. Bring to room temperature before serving.

3. Spread the butter over the hot corn.

Mexicali-Style Corn with Lime Butter and Cilantro

This dish brings back memories from my childhood when, once a week, my mom would serve up canned Mexicali corn, along with pork chops and applesauce. While I have to admit I still hold a place in my heart for the canned variety, making it from scratch with fresh ingredients wins out, hands down. Chilling the butter mixture before adding it to the hot ingredients is an important step because the butter coats the vegetables as it melts and gives the finished dish a creamy consistency.

Serves 4

4 tablespoons unsalted butter, slightly softened
Grated zest and juice of 1 lime
1 teaspoon honey
Kosher salt
2 tablespoons canola oil
1 small red onion, finely diced
1 jalapeño chile, finely diced

1 red bell pepper, finely diced
2 cloves garlic, finely chopped
Perfectly Grilled Corn (page 83), kernels removed from the cobs
Freshly ground black pepper
¼ cup coarsely chopped fresh cilantro leaves

1. Whisk together the butter, lime zest and juice, honey, and 1 teaspoon salt in a small bowl. Place in the refrigerator until firm, approximately 15 minutes, or for up to 1 day.

2. Heat the oil in a large sauté pan over high heat until it begins to shimmer. Add the onion, jalapeño, and bell pepper and cook until soft, 4 to 5 minutes. Add the garlic and cook for 30 seconds. Stir in the corn and cook until just heated through, 2 to 3 minutes.

3. Add the butter and stir until it just begins to melt and coats the mixture. Remove from the heat, season with salt and pepper, and add the cilantro.

Grilled Corn on the Cob with BBQ Butter

Corn on the cob is already such a traditional accompaniment to a summer barbecue that it makes perfect sense to take it just one step farther, and barbecue the corn! Grilling the ears gives corn a smoky edge to its sweetness, which is only heightened by a barbecue-flavored butter packed with intense cumin, chile powder, and paprika. Its deep, glistening color doesn't hurt that barbecue image, either.

Serves 4

2 tablespoons canola oil
½ small red onion, chopped
2 cloves garlic, chopped
1 tablespoon ancho chile powder
2 teaspoons Spanish paprika
1 teaspoon cumin seeds, toasted (see page 19)
½ teaspoon cayenne pepper

2 teaspoons molasses
12 tablespoons (1½ sticks) unsalted butter, slightly softened
1 teaspoon Worcestershire sauce
Kosher salt and freshly ground black pepper
Perfectly Grilled Corn (page 83)

1. Heat the oil in a medium sauté pan over high heat until almost smoking. Add the onion and cook until soft, 2 to 3 minutes. Add the garlic and cook for 30 seconds. Add the ancho powder, paprika, cumin, and cayenne and cook for 1 minute. Add ½ cup of water and the molasses and cook until the mixture thickens and the water has evaporated, about 5 minutes. Let cool slightly.

2. Put the butter in a food processor, add the spice mixture and Worcestershire sauce, and process until smooth. Season with salt and pepper. Scrape the mixture into a small bowl, cover, and refrigerate for at least 30 minutes or up to 2 days to allow the flavors to meld. Bring to room temperature before serving.

3. Spread the butter over the corn while the corn is hot.

Cuban-Style Corn

This is one of the wonders of south-of-the-border street food, and when traveling in those regions I'm tempted to eat it from every corner vendor I hear hawking the savory treat. I've seen corn prepared this way in Mexico, but I've consumed it the most during my visits to the Cuban neighborhoods of Miami. Traditionally, the mayonnaise is just a slick of rich glue to anchor a dash of chile powder, salt, crumbled cotija cheese, and a squeeze of fresh lime juice to each ear of corn. I prefer to mix up the mayonnaise with those ingredients (save for the cheese) along with garlic ahead of time so that all of those incredible flavors get a chance to meld before coating each kernel of corn. If you haven't tried this yet, the combination of grilled corn and mayonnaise may seem a little iffy, but after one bite, you'll see just how amazing it can be.

Serves 4

1½ cups mayonnaise
4 cloves garlic, finely chopped
2 tablespoons ancho chile powder
1 tablespoon fresh lime juice

½ teaspoon kosher salt
1½ cups grated cotija cheese
Perfectly Grilled Corn (page 83)
Grated zest of 2 limes

1. Whisk together the mayonnaise, garlic, ancho powder, lime juice, and salt in a medium bowl. Cover and refrigerate for at least 30 minutes or up to 8 hours before using.

2. Spread the cheese onto a large plate. Brush eat hot ear of corn with some of the garlic–red chile mayonnaise, then roll in the cheese, and sprinkle with lime zest. Serve immediately.

fruit

Grilled Bananas with Dulce de Leche Ice Cream and Cinnamon-Orange Sauce • Grilled Apricots with Greek Yogurt, Warm Honey, and Toasted Walnuts • Grilled Banana and Nutella Panini • Grilled Nectarines with Maple Crème Fraîche • Grilled Peaches Foster with Crème Fraîche • Grilled Peaches with Red Wine Syrup and Amaretto Cookies • Rum Raisin Pear Packets with Chocolate Sorbet • Grilled Pineapple with Grated Chocolate and Toasted Hazelnuts • Grilled Pineapple with Pound Cake and Rum-Caramel Sauce

Grilled fruit might seem like a novelty to some, but it shouldn't. The direct, searing heat of the grill can transform a piece of unremarkable fruit into one bursting with concentrated flavor. Fruit's makeup is pretty basic. It contains two components: sugar and water. Grilling reduces the water and caramelizes the natural sugars in minutes. The process is so simple; when you have the grill fired up for your main course, why not take care of dessert at the same time? A quick glaze or a scoop of ice cream and you're done! Some fruits also take well to savory preparations, so don't think grilled fruit necessarily has to be dessert-only. I especially love a salad of grilled peaches or nectarines with blue cheese.

Make sure to select fruits that are substantial enough to hold their shape and texture when grilled. I like to use pineapple and stone fruits such as peaches, nectarines, plums, and apricots. When grilling the latter, choose fruit that is just slightly underripe so that it doesn't fall apart. Don't worry about the flavor being underdeveloped; the grill takes care of that.

There are just a few simple rules to remember when grilling fruit. For starters, make sure that the fruit is solid enough to hold together on the grill. Then, to prevent it from sticking, you will need to brush just a touch of oil onto the flesh of the fruit—and no extra-virgin olive oil here. Choose an oil that is as neutral tasting as possible so that it doesn't impart any added flavor to the fruit. I always use canola oil. Finally—and this might be the most important rule of all—you have to start with a clean grill! The last thing you want is a piece of grilled fruit that tastes like last night's hamburgers. I am always a stickler about maintaining a clean grill and I brush the grates while they are still warm each and every time I use it. If you let that cooked-on food build up, it will be a whole afternoon's project as opposed to a few minutes of regular upkeep. This holds with everything you grill, but delicate, sweet fruit demands a clean grill more than any other ingredient.

Grilled Bananas with Dulce de Leche Ice Cream and Cinnamon-Orange Sauce

If you haven't tried grilling bananas, you definitely should. Keeping them partially in their skin while grilling keeps the bananas from falling apart on the grill. The combination of sweet, floral oranges and faintly spicy cinnamon elevates the humble banana to star status.

Serves 4

2 teaspoons grated orange zest
3 cups orange juice (not from concentrate)
2 tablespoons granulated sugar
2 tablespoons light brown sugar
½ teaspoon ground cinnamon

4 ripe bananas
2 tablespoons butter, melted, or canola oil
4 scoops dulce de leche or vanilla ice cream
2 tablespoons sliced almonds, toasted (see page 19; optional)

1. Combine the orange zest, juice, and granulated and brown sugars in a medium saucepan over high heat and simmer, stirring frequently, until reduced to 1 cup and thickened to a sauce consistency, about 15 minutes. Remove from the heat and stir in the ground cinnamon. Let cool slightly. (The sauce can be served warm or at room temperature.)

2. Heat your grill to medium-high.

3. Leaving the skin on, cut the bananas in half crosswise and then again lengthwise. Brush the cut side of the bananas with the butter and place them on the grill, cut side down. Grill until lightly golden brown, 2 to 3 minutes. Turn the bananas over and continue cooking, skin side down, until the skin begins to pull away from the banana, about 1 minute longer.

4. Remove the skins from the bananas and place 4 pieces into each serving bowl. Top with a large scoop of ice cream and drizzle with the cinnamon-orange syrup and toasted sliced almonds, if desired.

Grilled Apricots with Greek Yogurt, Warm Honey, and Toasted Walnuts

Fresh, ripe apricots are irresistible. Unfortunately, their season is so short that most people never have the opportunity to experience them and are only familiar with the dried variety. Make it a point to find some when they become available in May or June and try this recipe. Even though they are wonderful eaten raw, grilling them and topping them with cold, creamy Greek yogurt and warm honey puts them over the top and makes for an elegant dessert. If you can't find fresh apricots or they are out of season, substitute fresh nectarines, peaches, or plums. Don't let this recipe go to waste.

Serves 4

6 ripe apricots, halved and pitted
3 tablespoons canola oil
½ cup honey

¼ cup chopped walnuts, toasted (see page 19)
¾ cup Greek yogurt
Fresh mint sprigs, for garnish (optional)

1. Heat your grill to high.

2. Brush the apricots with the oil, place on the grill cut side down, and cook until golden brown and caramelized, about 2 minutes. Turn the apricots over and continue cooking until just warmed through, about 2 minutes longer.

3. While the apricots are cooking, combine the honey and walnuts in a small pan, place on the grates of the grill, and cook until heated through, about 3 minutes.

4. Remove the apricots from the grill and place 3 halves on each plate. Top each half with some of the yogurt and drizzle the honey-walnut mixture over the top. Garnish with a mint sprig, if desired.

Grilled Banana and Nutella Panini

Elvis had his peanut butter and banana sandwich and I have this. Now, I love peanut butter as much as the next American, but I am crazy about Nutella, an extremely rich and creamy chocolate and hazelnut spread from Italy. You can find Nutella in your grocery store keeping company, coincidentally, with the peanut butter.

Serves 4

2 ripe bananas
8 (½-inch-thick) slices French baguette
½ cup Nutella

8 tablespoons (1 stick) unsalted butter, softened
2 tablespoons confectioners' sugar

1. Put the bananas in a bowl and mash until smooth.

2. Lay out the slices of bread on a flat surface and spread each slice with some of the Nutella. Spread the mashed banana over 4 of the slices of bread and top with the other 4 slices, Nutella side down, to make 4 sandwiches.

3. Heat your grill to medium.

4. Spread one side of each sandwich with some of the butter and place on the grill, buttered side down. Grill until golden brown, about 2 minutes. Spread the remaining butter on the bread facing up, flip over, and continue grilling until golden brown, about 2 minutes. Remove from the grill and sprinkle with the confectioners' sugar. Serve immediately.

Grilled Nectarines with Maple Crème Fraîche

Nectarines are one of my favorite fruits for grilling. Not only does their firm texture hold up extremely well on the grill, but I also often find that nectarines have a subtle sour note beneath their sweetness, and I love the way heat brings nectarines' sweetness front and center. The tangy-sweet combination of maple syrup and crème fraîche makes a perfect topping for the grilled fruit, and a garnish of fresh berries is beautiful and delicious.

Serves 4

4 ripe nectarines, halved and pitted
2 tablepoons canola oil
Kosher salt and freshly ground black pepper
¾ cup crème fraîche or sour cream

3 tablespoons pure maple syrup
½ pint raspberries and blackberries for serving (optional)
Fresh mint sprigs for garnish (optional)

1. Heat your grill to high.

2. Brush the cut side of the nectarines with the oil and season with salt and pepper. Grill until golden brown, about 3 minutes. Turn over and continue grilling until just cooked through, about 3 minutes longer.

3. Transfer the nectarines, cut sides up, to 4 bowls. Whisk together the crème fraîche and maple syrup. Place a large dollop in the center of each nectarine half. Garnish with berries and mint, if desired.

Grilled Peaches Foster with Crème Fraîche

It's dessert as theater! Bananas Foster is the legendary flaming dessert first created at Brennan's Restaurant in New Orleans in the 1950s. While I love the spectacle of it all, the traditional recipe, which calls for bananas flambéed in rum and banana liqueur served over vanilla ice cream, can be a little cloyingly sweet for some people. The concept can be applied to several different fruits, so I use peaches in place of the bananas and bourbon in place of the sweet rum and liqueur. Crème fraîche is a refreshing, tangy alternative to ice cream, but feel free to use ice cream if desired.

Serves 4

8 tablespoons (1 stick) unsalted butter
½ cup packed light brown sugar
6 large slightly under-ripe peaches, halved and pitted
¼ cup canola oil

⅓ cup bourbon
¼ teaspoon ground cinnamon
⅛ teaspoon salt
½ cup chopped pecans, toasted (see page 19)
½ cup crème fraîche or sour cream

1. Heat your grill to high.

2. Place a medium saucepan on the grates of the grill, add the butter and brown sugar, and cook, stirring occasionally, until the sugar has melted and the mixture thickens slightly, about 5 minutes.

3. While the sauce is cooking, brush the cut sides of the peaches with the oil and place on the grill, cut side down. Grill until lightly golden brown and caramelized, 2 to 3 minutes. Turn the peaches over and continue grilling until just cooked through, 3 to 4 minutes longer. Remove to a cutting board and cut each half in half.

4. Remove the pan with the sauce from the heat and add the bourbon. Using a long lit match, ignite the bourbon and allow the flames to subside. Stir in the cinnamon, salt, and pecans.

5. Divide the peaches among 4 bowls and spoon some of the sauce over the peaches. Top with a large dollop of crème fraîche and serve immediately.

Grilled Peaches with Red Wine Syrup and Amaretto Cookies

A cinch to prepare, these luscious peaches are a fabulous finale for an Italian meal. Red wine reduces with sugar, vanilla, and licorice-flavored star anise to a complex, sweet, and glossy syrup to serve over grilled peaches. Crushed amaretto cookies add a nice, almost spicy, crunch to the dish. This is one of those dishes that you could pull out of your pantry with no notice—and no one will ever be the wiser. One note: try to use a dry red wine so that the syrup doesn't end up too sweet.

Serves 4

2 cups dry red wine
½ cup sugar
1 vanilla bean, split
1 star anise or 1 teaspoon fennel seeds

6 ripe peaches, halved and pitted
2 tablespoons canola oil
8 amaretto cookies, coarsely crushed
Fresh mint sprigs, for garnish (optional)

1. Combine the wine, sugar, vanilla bean, and star anise in a medium saucepan over high heat and cook, stirring occasionally, until reduced by half and the mixture is thickened, 8 to 10 minutes. Remove from the heat and let cool to room temperature. Discard the vanilla bean and star anise. The syrup can be made 1 day in advance and stored, covered, in the refrigerator. Bring to room temperature before serving.

2. Heat your grill to high.

3. Brush the cut sides of the peaches with the oil and place on the grill, cut side down. Grill until golden brown, about 2 minutes. Turn the peaches over and continue cooking until just heated through, 3 to 4 minutes longer.

4. Serve 3 peach halves per person on a plate. Drizzle with some of the red wine syrup, sprinkle with the cookies, and garnish with mint sprigs, if desired.

Rum Raisin Pear Packets with Chocolate Sorbet

There is something really comforting about warm pears and raisins flavored with rum, butter, and sugar. The only thing that could make it better is the addition of chocolate. If you are feeling extremely decadent, then by all means feel free to substitute chocolate ice cream for the sorbet; but the sorbet makes for a really satisfying and *healthy* option.

Serves 4

8 large firm-ripe Bosc or Anjou pears, peeled, cut into 8 wedges, and cored
⅓ cup raisins
8 tablespoons (1 stick) unsalted cold butter, cut into small pieces

8 tablespoons light brown sugar
½ cup dark rum
4 scoops chocolate sorbet

1. Heat your grill to medium.

2. Cut out four 12-inch squares of heavy duty aluminum foil. Divide the pears among the foil squares, placing them in the center. Divide the raisins, butter, brown sugar, and rum over the pears and then fold up the foil over the pears. Place the packets on the grill, close the cover, and cook until the pears are soft and the butter and sugar have melted, 12 to 15 minutes. Remove from the grill and let sit for 5 minutes.

3. Place 1 scoop of chocolate sorbet into each of 4 bowls. Open up the pear packets and pour the contents over the sorbet.

Grilled Pineapple with Grated Chocolate and Toasted Hazelnuts

This is my favorite kind of dessert to make—an extraordinarily easy one! But don't think that just because it's simple to prepare it's lacking in flavor; it's delicious, too. The heat of the grill caramelizes the pineapple's natural sugars, pumping up its flavors and giving it gorgeous grill marks. Just a small amount of chocolate provides a big impact as the shavings melt into the hot fruit. Toasted hazelnuts add a nice crunch factor and a rich nutty flavor. And besides, you can't resist the classic flavor combination of chocolate and hazelnuts.

Serves 4

1 medium pineapple, peeled, cut into ½-inch slices, and cored
¼ cup canola oil
4 ounces bittersweet chocolate, finely grated

⅓ cup coarsely chopped hazelnuts, toasted (see page 19)
Freshly whipped cream (see note), for serving (optional)

1. Heat your grill to high.

2. Brush the pineapple on both sides with the oil and place on the grill. Grill until golden brown and caramelized on both sides, about 6 minutes.

3. Remove the pineapple from the grill and cut each slice into quarters. Divide among 4 bowls and immediately sprinkle the pineapple with the chocolate and hazelnuts. Top with a large dollop of whipped cream, if desired.

To prepare freshly whipped cream
Combine 1 cup cold heavy cream, 2 tablespoons granulated sugar, and 1 teaspoon pure vanilla extract in a bowl and beat with a large balloon whisk or hand-held mixer until soft peaks form

Grilled Pineapple with Pound Cake and Rum-Caramel Sauce

While I was growing up, my mother would make pineapple upside-down cake, normally using a boxed yellow cake mix and canned pineapple. While I have fond memories of that dessert with the maraschino cherries on top, I have no desire to whip up a cake batter, bake it in an oven, and then risk third-degree burns trying to invert it onto a platter. You don't have to, either. For this recipe all you have to do is pick up a store-bought pound cake, slice up a fresh pineapple, whisk together a quick caramel sauce (heck, you could even heat up a store-bought variety and just add a little rum), *and* fire up the grill.

Serves 4 to 8

2 tablespoons unsalted butter
¾ cup packed dark brown sugar
2 tablespoons dark rum
½ cup heavy cream
1 small pineapple, peeled, sliced into
   ½-inch-thick slices, and cored

¼ cup canola oil
1 (9-inch) loaf store-bought pound cake,
   cut into ½-inch-thick slices
Freshly whipped cream (see page 105), for
   serving (optional)
Maraschino cherries, for garnish (optional)

1. Melt the butter in a small saucepan over high heat, add the brown sugar and rum, and cook, whisking, until the sugar has melted and the mixture is smooth. Whisk in the heavy cream and cook until heated through and slightly thickened; about 2 minutes. Transfer the mixture to a bowl and keep warm.

2. Heat your grill to high.

3. Brush the pineapple on both sides with the oil and place on the grill. Grill until golden brown and caramelized on both sides, about 6 minutes.

4. While the pineapple is grilling, place the pound cake on the grill and grill until lightly golden brown on both sides, about 1 minute. Set each slice of pound cake on a serving plate.

5. Transfer the pineapple to a cutting board and cut into chunks.

6. Top each piece of pound cake with some of the pineapple and drizzle with the rum-caramel sauce. Top with a dollop of whipped cream and a maraschino cherry, if desired.

lamb

Grilled Lamb Chops with Garlic and Mustard • Grilled Baby Lamb Chops with Balsamic-Honey Glaze and Mint Pesto • Grilled Lamb Chops with Rosemary Salt and Black Olive Sauce • Spicy Lamb and Orzo Salad • Grilled Lamb with Greek Spinach Pita Salad • Grilled Lamb Loin with Pomegranate-Horseradish Glaze • Lamb Chops with Fresh Provençal Herbs, Arugula, and Mustard Vinaigrette • Grilled Lamb Sausage Souvlaki with Red Pepper Yogurt Sauce • Grilled Lamb with Green Pea Sauce and Mint Vinaigrette

Americans don't eat as much lamb as they do other meats, but it is incredibly popular in Mediterranean, Middle Eastern, and Asian cuisines. Lamb, while far from gamey, does have a distinctive and pronounced flavor and is particularly suited to the bold seasonings favored by those cultures. I like to prepare it Greek style, with tons of garlic and pungent herbs, or play up its natural sweetness in a Moroccan-inspired dish laced with pomegranate. On the flip side, the cuts of lamb that I like to use on the grill, such as tenderloin and rib chops, are also quite delicate and pair beautifully with tender spring vegetables. Refined rib chops and tenderloin are natural choices for an elegant, romantic meal for their impressive presentation factor and delicious taste. Although the cost of such cuts may be somewhat high, it's definitely worthwhile for a special meal.

Traditionally, lamb ushered in the spring, gracing most Easter and Passover dinner tables. You might still see "spring lamb" advertised around those holidays, but you can find lamb—fresh and frozen, domestically raised and from Australia and New Zealand—available year-round. American lamb is grain-fed and is more tender and milder in flavor than the grass-fed Australian and New Zealand lamb. Cut for cut, American lamb is also much larger. I prefer domestic lamb, but if faced with a choice, I'd always select fresh over frozen, regardless of its origin.

Lamb is graded on its degree of marbling, just like beef. Very little prime lamb is available, but the choice lamb on the market can be very good, especially because lamb needs significantly less marbling than beef to be tender and juicy. To ensure the best possible texture and flavor, I never like to grill my lamb past medium, though I think medium-rare is best. When buying lamb, look for moist, reddish bones, light red meat, and white fat. Dry bones, darker meat, and yellowing fat are indicators of advanced age.

Grilled Lamb Chops with Garlic and Mustard

This garlic-mustard mixture is almost like a wet rub, without a lot of oil; the mustard not only acts as a crucial flavoring but also helps as an anchor to keep all of the other flavor components adhered to the lamb. I call for two varieties of mustard here: whole-grain for its robust taste and look, and smooth Dijon for its sharpness. The rest of the ingredients are distinct yet all in perfect balance: smoky paprika and fresh thyme, sweet honey and salty soy sauce, and mellow olive oil and acidic vinegar. As for the garlic, it'd be a totally lesser dish without it!

Serves 4

¼ cup whole-grain mustard
2 tablespoons Dijon mustard
3 cloves garlic, finely chopped
2 tablespoons red wine vinegar
1 tablespoon low-sodium soy sauce
1 tablespoon olive oil
1 tablespoon honey

1 tablespoon finely chopped fresh thyme leaves
2 teaspoons Spanish paprika
Coarsely ground black pepper
12 (3-ounce) baby lamb chops, frenched
Kosher salt

1. Heat your grill to high.

2. Whisk together both of the mustards, the garlic, vinegar, soy sauce, oil, honey, thyme, paprika, and ¼ teaspoon pepper in a medium bowl. Pour half of the mixture into a second bowl and set aside for serving.

3. Season the chops on both sides with salt. Brush each chop with some of the mustard mixture and place on the grill, mustard side down. Grill until golden brown and slightly charred, 2 to 3 minutes. Flip the chops over, brush with more of the mustard mixture, and continue grilling to medium-rare, 2 to 3 minutes longer.

4. Remove from the grill, brush with the reserved glaze, tent with foil, and let rest for 5 minutes before serving.

Grilled Baby Lamb Chops with Balsamic-Honey Glaze and Mint Pesto

Just in case you were thinking it, let me tell you that lamb with mint is not over-done—at least in this case. It's a classic pairing for a reason. Mint's bright, herbaceous taste is the perfect foil for intensely flavored lamb. But this mint pesto couldn't be any farther from the insipid mint jelly you might be thinking of. It's fresh and savory, pungent with garlic, and rich with Parmesan cheese and pine nuts. This delicious pesto is just the right condiment for the simple, tangy-sweet balsamic-honey glazed lamb.

Serves 4

½ cup aged balsamic vinegar
¼ cup honey
Kosher salt and freshly ground black pepper

12 (3-ounce) baby lamb chops, frenched
2 tablespoons olive oil
Mint Pesto (recipe follows)

1. Heat your grill to high.

2. Whisk together the vinegar and honey in a small bowl and season with salt and pepper. Pour half of the mixture into a separate bowl and set aside for serving.

3. Brush the chops on both sides with the oil and season with salt and pepper. Place the chops on the grill and cook for 2 to 3 minutes, or until golden brown and slightly charred. Turn over, brush with some of the balsamic-honey glaze, and continue grilling for 2 minutes longer for medium-rare.

4. Remove from the grill, brush with the reserved glaze, tent with foil, and let rest for 5 minutes. Serve 3 chops per person and top each with a few teaspoons of the mint pesto.

Mint Pesto

Makes approximately ¾ cup

1½ cups tightly packed freshly flat-leaf parsley
   leaves
1 cup tightly packed fresh mint leaves
1 clove garlic
2 tablespoons pine nuts

⅓ cup extra-virgin olive oil
3 tablespoons freshly grated Parmigiano-
   Reggiano cheese
Kosher salt and freshly ground black pepper

Combine the parsley, mint, garlic, and pine nuts in a food processor and process
until coarsely chopped. With the motor running, slowly add the oil and process until
smooth. Add the cheese, season with salt and pepper, and process for a few seconds to combine. Scrape the pesto into a bowl. The pesto can be covered and refrigerated for up to 2 hours. Bring to room temperature before serving.

Grilled Lamb Chops with Rosemary Salt and Black Olive Sauce

Making your own flavored salts is easy, and I love the intense flavor they give to meat and fish. You can use just about any herb, so if you aren't a big fan of rosemary, feel free to substitute fresh thyme or oregano for this particular recipe. To save time, you can make the salt by just mixing together the finely chopped herbs and salt, but making it in a food processor releases the oils in the herbs and adds even more flavor to the salt. Make extra and store it in an airtight container to have on hand anytime you cook.

Serves 4

¼ cup kosher salt
2 tablespoons fresh rosemary leaves
8 (4-ounce) double-thick bone-in lamb chops

2 tablespoons olive oil
Freshly ground black pepper
Black Olive Sauce (recipe follows)

1. Heat your grill to high.

2. Combine the salt and rosemary in a food processor and process until combined.

3. Brush the chops on both sides with the oil and season with a few teaspoons of the salt mixture and some pepper. Place on the grill and grill until golden brown and slightly charred, 3 to 4 minutes. Flip the chops over and continue grilling to medium-rare, 2 to 3 minutes longer.

4. Remove from the grill, tent with foil, and let rest for 5 minutes before serving. Top each chop with a dollop of the black olive sauce, and serve the remaining sauce on the side.

Black Olive Sauce

Makes ⅔ cup

½ cup mayonnaise
Grated zest of 1 lemon
2 teaspoons fresh lemon juice
2 anchovy fillets, drained

2 cloves garlic, chopped
12 pitted Niçoise olives
¼ teaspoon kosher salt
¼ teaspoon freshly ground black pepper

Combine the mayonnaise, zest, juice, anchovies, and garlic in a food processor and process until smooth. Add the olives, salt, and pepper and pulse a few times just to incorporate the olives, not to puree them. Cover and refrigerate for at least 30 minutes or up to 8 hours before serving.

Spicy Lamb and Orzo Salad

Five-spice powder includes cinnamon, cloves, fennel seeds, star anise, and Szechwan peppercorns, and while it might sound like an odd combination, the flavors really complement each other. It is used in many Asian dishes and you can find it in the spice section of most supermarkets.

Serves 4

¼ cup plus 2 tablespoons canola oil
1 tablespoon five-spice powder
4 cloves garlic, finely chopped
1½ pounds lamb tenderloin
Kosher salt
3 tablespoons rice wine vinegar
1 tablespoon low sodium soy sauce

2 teaspoons toasted sesame oil
2 teaspoons sugar
2 Thai red chiles or 1 Fresno chile,
  thinly sliced
12 ounces orzo
3 green onions, thinly sliced
¼ cup chopped fresh cilantro leaves

1. Whisk together ¼ cup of the oil, the five-spice powder, and garlic in a medium baking dish, add the lamb and turn to coat in the mixture. Cover and refrigerate for at least 1 hour and up to 4 hours.

2. Whisk together the vinegar, soy sauce, sesame oil, sugar, chiles, and remaining 2 tablespoons canola oil in a large bowl and let sit while you prepare the orzo.

3. Bring a large pot of salted water to a boil. Add the orzo and cook until just tender, approximately 7 minutes. Drain well, place in the bowl with the dressing, add the green onions and cilantro and mix until combined. Let sit at room temperature while you cook the lamb. Can be made 8 hours in advance and refrigerated. Serve at room temperature or cold.

4. Heat your grill to high.

5. Remove the lamb from the marinade and season with salt. Place the tenderloins on the grill and cook until golden brown and slightly charred, 3 to 4 minutes. Turn over and continue grilling for 2 to 3 minutes for medium-rare doneness. Remove from the grill and let rest for 5 minutes before slicing into ¼-inch-thick slices. Transfer the orzo to a large platter and top with the sliced lamb.

Grilled Lamb with Greek Spinach Pita Salad

Lamb, spinach, feta, lemon, oregano, dill—these are ingredients you'll always find on a Greek menu. I am enamored of Greek food because of all of its bold flavors, and I definitely put those to work in this dish. You might not think of lamb as being particularly light, but this dish manages to be just that with its fresh, crunchy salad base. Crisp, grilled pita bread serves as an edible salad plate and makes for a really fun presentation.

Serves 4

Lamb
6 tablespoons olive oil
4 cloves garlic, coarsely chopped
2 tablespoons chopped fresh oregano leaves
1½ pounds lamb tenderloin, trimmed of fat
Kosher salt and freshly ground black pepper
4 pocketless pita breads

Salad
2 tablespoons fresh lemon juice
1 tablespoon red wine vinegar

2 tablespoons chopped fresh dill, plus more
   for garnish
Kosher salt and freshly ground black pepper
2 teaspoons honey
½ cup extra-virgin olive oil
6 ounces baby spinach
½ English cucumber, sliced
2 plum tomatoes, sliced
¼ cup Kalamata olives, pitted and chopped
4 ounces feta cheese, crumbled (1 cup)

1. To marinate the lamb, whisk together 4 tablespoons of the olive oil, the garlic, and oregano in a medium baking dish. Add the lamb and turn to coat. Cover and let marinate in the refrigerator for at least 1 hour and up to 24 hours.

2. Heat your grill to high.

3. Remove the lamb from the marinade and season with salt and pepper on both sides. Place on the grill and grill until golden brown and slightly charred, 3 to 4 minutes. Turn the lamb over and continue grilling to medium-rare, 2 to 3 minutes longer. Remove to a cutting board, tent with foil, and let rest for 5 minutes before slicing into ½-inch-thick slices.

4. While the lamb is resting, brush each pita on both sides with the remaining 2 tablespoons oil and season with salt and pepper. Grill until golden brown and slightly crisp, approximately 30 seconds per side.

5. To make the salad, whisk together the lemon juice, vinegar, dill, salt and pepper to taste, and the honey in a large bowl. Slowly whisk in the extra-virgin olive oil until emulsified. Add the spinach, cucumber, tomatoes, olives, and feta to the bowl and toss to combine.

6. Top each pita with some of the salad and top with several slices of the lamb.

Grilled Lamb Loin with Pomegranate-Horseradish Glaze

This dish is simply stunning: the meat is glossy brown on the outside and pink inside, and the whole thing is crowned with a jewel-like pomegranate relish. Pomegranate molasses, which is most commonly used in Middle Eastern cuisine, is made from pomegranate juice that has been reduced to a thick and viscous syrup. Its intense color and sweetness make for a gorgeous, delicious glaze. Horseradish's bite keeps the glaze from being cloying, as does Dijon mustard.

Serves 4

½ cup pomegranate molasses
2 tablespoons prepared horseradish, drained
2 tablespoons Dijon mustard
Kosher salt and freshly ground black pepper

2 pounds lamb tenderloin
3 tablespoons canola oil
Pomegranate Relish (recipe follows)

1. Whisk together the pomegranate molasses, horseradish, and mustard in a small bowl and season with salt and pepper. Let sit at room temperature for 30 minutes before using. The glaze can be made 1 day in advance, covered and refrigerated, and brought to room temperature before using.

2. Heat your grill to high.

3. Brush the lamb with the oil and season with salt and pepper. Place on the grill and cook until golden brown and slightly charred, 2 to 3 minutes. Flip the lamb over, brush with some of the glaze, and continue grilling for 3 to 4 minutes longer for medium-rare.

4. Brush with the remaining glaze, remove from the grill, tent with foil, and let rest for 5 minutes. Slice into 1-inch-thick slices. Serve on a platter and top each piece with some of the relish.

Pomegranate Relish

Makes approximately ¾ cup

Seeds of 1 pomegranate
1 small red onion, finely chopped
1 jalapeño chile, finely diced

¼ cup finely chopped fresh flat-leaf parsley leaves
Kosher salt

Combine the pomegranate seeds, onion, jalapeño, and parsley in a small bowl and season with salt. Let sit at room temperature for 30 minutes or up to 2 hours before serving.

Lamb Chops with Fresh Provençal Herbs, Arugula, and Mustard Vinaigrette

Herbes de Provence is a fragrant mix of herbs from the Provence region of France. Although I think the dried version is good when added to long-cooking braised dishes, I prefer a livelier taste when grilling and make my own mix of the same fresh herbs. Since the marinade for the lamb is centered around French flavors, it only seemed right to serve it with a vinaigrette based on another of France's greatest flavors: Dijon mustard. See photograph on page 108.

Serves 4

2 tablespoons finely chopped fresh thyme leaves
2 tablespoons finely chopped fresh basil leaves
1 tablespoon finely chopped fresh rosemary leaves
1 tablespoon finely chopped fresh marjoram or oregano leaves
1 fresh or dried bay leaf
¾ cup olive oil
8 (3-ounce) baby lamb chops, trimmed of fat
Kosher salt and freshly ground black pepper
6 ounces baby arugula
Mustard Vinaigrette (recipe follows)

1. Whisk together the thyme, basil, rosemary, marjoram, bay leaf, and oil in a large baking dish. Add the lamb and turn to coat with the mixture. Cover and refrigerate for at least 1 hour and up to 8 hours.

2. Heat your grill to high.

3. Remove the lamb from the marinade and season on both sides with salt and pepper. Grill until golden brown and cooked to medium, 2 to 3 minutes per side.

4. Arrange the arugula on a large platter and immediately top with the lamb chops and drizzle with the mustard vinaigrette. The heat from the lamb will wilt the arugula slightly.

Mustard Vinaigrette

Makes approximately ¾ cup

¼ cup white wine vinegar
1 heaping tablespoon Dijon mustard
2 cloves garlic, finely chopped
1 teaspoon honey
¼ teaspoon kosher salt
¼ teaspoon freshly ground black pepper
½ cup extra-virgin olive oil

Whisk together the vinegar, mustard, garlic, honey, salt, and pepper in a small bowl. Slowly whisk in the oil until emulsified. The vinaigrette can be made a day in advance, covered, and refrigerated. Bring to room temperature before serving.

Grilled Lamb Sausage Souvlaki with Red Pepper Yogurt Sauce

Lamb souvlaki served up in a pita with yogurt sauce is pretty standard Greek fare, found everywhere from restaurants in Athens, Greece, to food carts on New York City streets. This version is more along the lines of something that you might find at my Spanish-Mediterranean restaurant, Bolo. Spicy lamb merguez sausage and slightly sweet and smoky piquillo peppers are traditional Spanish ingredients, but they find themselves right at home in this flavorful sandwich.

Serves 4 to 6

½ cup plus 2 tablespoons olive oil
6 cloves garlic, chopped
1 medium yellow onion, coarsely chopped
2 tablespoons chopped fresh oregano leaves,
  plus more whole leaves for garnish
2 pounds lamb tenderloin, cut into 1-inch cubes
1 pound merguez sausages
2 red bell peppers

1 large red onion, cut crosswise into
  ½-inch-thick slices
Kosher salt and freshly ground black pepper
Wooden skewers, soaked in water for
  30 minutes
8 pocket pita breads
Red Pepper–Yogurt Sauce (recipe follows)

120

1. Whisk together 1 cup of the oil, the garlic, chopped yellow onion, and oregano in a large bowl; add the lamb; and toss to coat. Cover and marinate in the refrigerator for at least 1 hour or up to 8 hours.

2. Heat your grill to high.

3. Grill the sausages until golden brown on all sides and just cooked through, 10 to 12 minutes.

4. While grilling the sausage, brush the bell pepper and red onion slices with the remaining 2 tablespoons oil and season with salt and pepper. Grill the onion for 3 to 4 minutes on each side until slightly charred and just cooked through. Grill the pepper, turning onto all sides, until charred, 8 to 10 minutes. Remove from the grill, transfer to a bowl, cover, and let sit for 10 minutes before peeling, coring, seeding, and slicing.

5. Remove the sausage from the grill, let rest for 5 minutes, and cut into 1-inch pieces. Thread the lamb and sausage onto the skewers and season with salt and pepper.

6. Grill the skewers for 2 minutes per side, or until the lamb is golden brown and cooked to medium-rare. Grill the pita on both sides for about 20 seconds to warm through.

7. Slice off 1 inch from the top of each pita. Remove the lamb and sausage from the skewers and stuff into the pita. Add some onion and peppers, drizzle with some of the yogurt sauce, and garnish with oregano.

Red Pepper–Yogurt Sauce

Makes approximately 1¾ cups

1½ cups Greek yogurt
4 piquillo peppers or 1 large grilled red bell
   pepper (see opposite)
4 cloves garlic, coarsely chopped

2 teaspoons grated lemon zest
2 teaspoons chopped fresh oregano leaves
Kosher salt and freshly ground black pepper

Combine the yogurt, peppers, garlic, lemon zest, and oregano in a blender and blend until smooth. Season with salt and pepper to taste and transfer to a small bowl. The sauce will keep, covered in the refrigerator, for up to 1 day.

Grilled Lamb with Green Pea Sauce and Mint Vinaigrette

The sauce is my version of skordalia, a traditional Greek dip made with potatoes, bread, and plenty of garlic. I'd never get rid of the garlic, but making it with green peas instead of the potatoes and bread adds a lighter texture that is perfect for warm-weather eating. Peas, mint, and lamb—you can't help but feel like you're welcoming springtime in with this classic combination. The skordalia is really tasty and you might want to make extra to have on hand as a dip for pita bread and fresh veggies.

Serves 4

1 (10-ounce) package frozen peas
6 cloves garlic
1 serrano chile, grilled (see page 120), peeled, seeded, and chopped
Grated zest of 1 lemon
Juice of 1 lemon
2 teaspoons honey

¾ cup extra-virgin olive oil
¼ cup chopped fresh flat-leaf parsley leaves
Kosher salt and freshly ground black pepper
1½ pounds lamb tenderloin
2 tablespoons olive oil
Mint Vinaigrette (recipe follows)

1. Cook the peas according to package directions. Drain well.

2. Combine the peas, garlic, serrano chile, lemon zest and juice, and honey in a food processor and process until coarsely chopped. With the motor running, slowly add the extra-virgin olive oil until emulsified. Add the parsley, season with salt and pepper, and pulse a few times. Scrape into a bowl. The pea sauce can be made 4 hours in advance and refrigerated. Bring to room temperature before serving.

3. Heat your grill to high.

4. Brush the lamb with the olive oil and season with salt and pepper. Place on the grill and cook until golden brown and slightly charred, 2 to 3 minutes. Flip the lamb over and continue grilling for 3 to 4 minutes longer for medium-rare.

5. Remove from the grill, tent with foil, and let rest for 5 minutes before slicing into 1-inch-thick slices. Place a large dollop of the pea sauce in the center of 4 large plates. Arrange lamb slices around the sauce and drizzle with some of the vinaigrette.

Mint Vinaigrette

Makes approximately 1 cup

3 tablespoons white wine vinegar
1 tablespoon fresh lemon juice
2 teaspoons Dijon mustard
1 teaspoon honey

½ teaspoon kosher salt
¼ teaspoon freshly ground black pepper
½ cup canola oil
¼ cup packed fresh mint leaves

Combine the vinegar, lemon juice, mustard, honey, salt, and pepper in a blender and blend until smooth. With the motor running, slowly add the oil until emulsified. Add the mint leaves and blend until just combined. Do not blend until totally smooth; flecks of mint should still appear in the vinaigrette. The vinaigrette can be made up to 1 hour in advance and kept at room temperature.

lobster

Perfectly Grilled Whole Lobsters • Perfectly Grilled Lobster Tails • Grilled Lobster Tails with Fra Diavolo Vinaigrette • Grilled Lobster Cocktails with Coconut Milk • Grilled Lobster and Avocado Cocktails • Grilled Lobster with Creamy Chile-Garlic Vinaigrette • Lobster Taco • Grilled Lobster Rolls with Lemon–Black Pepper Mayonnaise • Grilled Lobster Tails with White Clam Sauce

I've heard lobster was once so plentiful that it was served at poorhouses and used as fertilizer. Not so now; pricey lobster has become a luxury ingredient. I have no problem seeing its allure, no matter what the price. Its intensely flavored, thick, and meaty flesh is delicious. I can't imagine a trip to the New England shore without a lobster salad roll or, even better, whole steamed lobster with drawn butter. To some, that's where lobster ends, but not for me. I happen to think that two of summer's greatest joys are the outdoor grill and lobster, and introducing one to the other—magic. A special meal of grilled lobster is one that you and your guests will both savor at the table and remember for a long time.

There are two types of lobster on the American market, the clawed lobster—which most of us are used to seeing—and the spiny or rock lobster. The clawed lobster is a cold-water animal and has—you guessed it—two claws. The spiny lobster lives in warm water, is not quite as firm as the clawed, and has a milder flavor. The spiny lobster has a darker shell than the orange-and-black-shelled clawed lobster and lacks the distinctive pincer and crusher claws of its cousin. I tend to prefer the clawed lobster over any other variety.

Now, the only good way to get a fresh whole lobster is to buy (or order) it live. A lobster packed in damp newspaper or, even better yet, seaweed will stay alive for a couple of days if refrigerated, but still, you want to start with the real deal. If you buy it yourself, go to a place that you think does a brisk business to ensure a high product turnover rate. You definitely don't want one that has been sitting in the tank for a while. Pick it up. The lobster should be lively, curling its tail and waving its claws. For the home cook, I recommend parboiling the lobster before grilling. It's easy and helps maintain an evenly cooked and tender end result.

Another option for easy grilling is lobster tail. The fish market may sell lobsters missing one or both of their claws (these are called culls) at a discounted price; or, as an even less expensive option, you could try frozen lobster tails. Just defrost before using and you're good to go. One note: many of the frozen lobster tails out there are from the less desirable (though certainly not bad) spiny lobster. I think it's worth your time and your money to try to ascertain which type of lobster the frozen tails came from and get the clawed variety if at all possible.

Perfectly Grilled Whole Lobsters

I love lobster, steamed, broiled, or roasted; but it will come as no surprise that I have a special affinity for it grilled. Yes, it takes a little work, but the payoff makes it all worthwhile. Whole lobsters need to be partially cooked before grilling. (If you tried to cook a raw lobster on the grill it would be too tough and the outside would burn before the inside was cooked.) You can eat your grilled lobsters with melted butter or a squeeze of lemon, or chop up the meat and use it for lobster rolls (page 135), lobster cocktails (pages 130 and 132), or anything else your heart or stomach desires.

Serves 4

Kosher salt
4 (2-pound) live lobsters

½ cup canola oil
Freshly ground black pepper

1. In a large pot of boiling salted water, boil the lobsters in batches for 10 to 12 minutes (they will be about three-quarters done). Drain well and let cool slightly. The lobsters can be parboiled a few hours in advance, covered, and kept refrigerated. Bring to room temperature before grilling.

2. Heat your grill to high.

3. Split each lobster lengthwise down the underside with a heavy knife, taking care not to cut through the back shell, so that the lobster is still in one piece but the inside is exposed. Brush the cut sides of the lobsters with the oil and season with salt and pepper.

4. Place the lobsters cut side down on the grill and cook until lightly charred and heated through, 4 to 6 minutes.

Perfectly Grilled Lobster Tails

Lobster tails are a fantastic grilling option. To start with, some people may be a bit squeamish when it comes to dealing with live lobster and buying just the tails takes away that worry. The tails are nicely portioned, simple to prepare on the grill, and they have the added bonus of being most people's favorite section to boot! In addition, frozen lobster tails are often available in the freezer section of better supermarkets, making them an economical and easy way to bring a luxurious item to your table. If using frozen lobster tails, you will need to defrost them first. This is best done by moving them to your refrigerator for eight to ten hours before cooking. If you are looking for a faster method, place the tails in a sealed plastic bag, submerge them in a bowl of cool water, and put the whole set up in the refrigerator for an hour or two.

Serves 4

Kosher salt
8 (8-ounce) lobster tails, in the shell

½ cup canola oil
Freshly ground black pepper

1. Bring a large pot of salted water to a boil. Add the lobster tails and boil for 6 minutes. Remove and drain well.

2. Heat your grill to high.

3. Split each lobster tail lengthwise down the underside with a heavy knife, taking care not to cut through the back shell so that the lobster is still in one piece but the inside is exposed. Brush the flesh side of each lobster tail with the oil and season with salt and pepper. Place the tails, flesh side down, on the grill and grill until slightly charred, 2 to 3 minutes. Flip over and continue grilling until just cooked through, 2 to 3 minutes.

Grilled Lobster Tails
with Fra Diavolo Vinaigrette

Fra Diavolo, which translated means brother devil in Italian, is a spicy tomato sauce most commonly eaten with seafood and pasta in southern Italy. The original sauce is normally cooked on the stove for an hour or so until thickened. To make it simpler and to avoid using the stove, I decided to make a quick and easy recipe that is more vinaigrette than sauce, and can be mixed up in the blender in a few minutes. The key to making this vinaigrette as flavorful as the cooked version is to use really, really, ripe tomatoes; in fact, I would even suggest overripe tomatoes.

Serves 4

3 very ripe large beefsteak tomatoes, halved, seeded, and coarsely chopped
2 cloves garlic, smashed
¼ teaspoon red chile flakes, or more to taste
2 teaspoons honey
½ to ⅓ cup extra-virgin olive oil (depending on how juicy the tomatoes are)

2 teaspoons chopped fresh thyme leaves
3 tablespoons chopped fresh flat-leaf parsley leaves plus 2 tablespoons whole leaves, for garnish
Kosher salt and freshly ground black pepper
Perfectly Grilled Lobster Tails (opposite)

1. Combine the tomatoes, garlic, red chile flakes, and honey in a blender and blend until smooth. With the motor running, add the olive oil and blend until thickened. Add the thyme, chopped parsley, and salt and pepper to taste and pulse a few times until incorporated. Transfer the sauce to a bowl. The sauce can be made up to 30 minutes before serving and kept at room temperature.

2. Remove the lobster tails from the grill, spoon the vinaigrette over them, and garnish with the whole parsley leaves.

Grilled Lobster Cocktails with Coconut Milk

At Bar Americain, I serve this cocktail with crabmeat instead of lobster, but I also think grilled lobster works perfectly. This is a Caribbean-inspired dish, from the fresh seafood to the coconut milk down to the fried plantain garnish. Not only does diced mango add a bright spot of color, but its sweetness also reinforces the natural sweet taste of the lobster.

Serves 4

1 (14.5-ounce) can unsweetened coconut milk
3 tablespoons habanero hot sauce (such as El Yucateco), or more to taste
Juice of 2 limes
2 tablespoons honey
1 teaspoon kosher salt
¼ teaspoon freshly ground black pepper
2 (2-pound) lobsters, cooked as for Perfectly Grilled Whole Lobsters (page 127), meat removed from shells, claws coarsely chopped

1 small ripe mango, peeled, pitted, and finely diced
¼ cup chopped fresh cilantro leaves, plus more for garnish
4 endive spears, thinly sliced
4 radicchio leaves, thinly sliced
1 (3-ounce) bag fried plantain chips or tortilla chips, optional

1. Whisk together the coconut milk, hot sauce, lime juice, honey, salt, and pepper in a large bowl. Cover and let sit at room temperature for 15 minutes.

2. Gently fold in the chopped lobster, mango, cilantro, endive, and radicchio and stir to combine. Using a slotted spoon, divide the mixture among 4 martini glasses or bowls. Top each serving with half a lobster tail and garnish around the perimeter with 3 to 4 plantain chips and cilantro.

Grilled Lobster and
Avocado Cocktails

I serve this cocktail at my restaurant Bar Americain. Presented in individual glasses, it makes such an elegant appetizer. Horseradish and Tabasco sauce are two important components of a traditional seafood cocktail sauce, but this tomato-free dressing is slightly more sophisticated. Chopped watercress lends a fresh crunchy bite to the otherwise smooth dish. (See photograph on page 131.)

Serves 4

½ cup fresh lime juice (about 4 to 5 limes)
2 teaspoons honey
2 tablespoons prepared horseradish, drained
1 tablespoon Worcestershire sauce
1 teaspoon Tabasco sauce
1 tablespoon finely chopped fresh tarragon
    leaves
Kosher salt and freshly ground black pepper

2 (2-pound) lobsters, cooked as for Perfectly
    Grilled Whole Lobsters (page 127), meat
    removed and coarsely chopped
1 ripe Hass avocado, peeled, pitted, and
    finely diced
1 small red onion, halved and thinly sliced
¾ cup chopped watercress

Whisk together the lime juice, honey, horseradish, Worcestershire, Tabasco, tarragon, and salt and pepper to taste in a medium bowl. Add the lobster, avocado, and red onion. The cocktail can be made up to 2 hours in advance and refrigerated. Add the watercress just before serving. Spoon into 4 martini glasses or bowls.

Grilled Lobster with
Creamy Chile-Garlic Vinaigrette

I consider this my version of an upscale iceberg wedge salad with Thousand Island that I always used to order at restaurants when I was a child. Ancho powder and garlic add a little spice to the vinaigrette, and romaine has the same crunch factor as—but more flavor than—iceberg lettuce. Make sure the lettuce and vinaigrette are properly chilled before serving. They provide a wonderful contrast to the warm lobster meat.

Serves 4

½ cup mayonnaise
2 tablespoons finely chopped fresh cilantro leaves
1 tablespoon red wine vinegar
2 tablespoons olive oil
2 tablespoons fresh lemon juice
2 tablespoons Dijon mustard
2 cloves garlic, finely chopped

2 tablespoons ancho chile powder
Kosher salt and freshly ground black pepper
1 head of romaine lettuce, finely shredded
2 (2-pound) lobsters, cooked as for Perfectly Grilled Whole Lobsters (page 127), meat removed and coarsely chopped
3 tablespoons finely chopped fresh chives

1. Whisk together the mayonnaise, cilantro, vinegar, oil, lemon juice, mustard, garlic, and ancho powder in a medium bowl and season with salt and pepper. Cover and refrigerate for at least 30 minutes or up to 4 hours before serving to allow the vinaigrette to chill and the flavors to meld.

2. Place the lettuce in a large bowl, add the vinaigrette, and toss to coat. Divide the lettuce among 4 plates and top with some of the lobster meat. Garnish with the fresh chives.

Lobster Taco

It should come as no surprise that I love tacos and fill them with everything from chicken and beef to lamb, shrimp, and white fish. So why not lobster? Lobster's meaty texture is a perfect option for those friends who don't eat meat and satisfying enough for those who do. Since the salsa is not cooked, make sure to use the freshest, ripest tomatoes you can find for the best flavor possible. If you aren't a fan of watercress or can't find it at your market, feel free to substitute shredded white cabbage, romaine lettuce, or fresh spinach leaves for some crunch.

Serves 4

Juice of 2 limes
2 teaspoons pureed chipotle chiles in adobo
2 teaspoons honey
¼ cup extra-virgin olive oil
2 large ripe beefsteak tomatoes, halved, seeded, and diced
3 tablespoons coarsely chopped fresh mint leaves

1 tablespoon coarsely chopped fresh cilantro leaves
Kosher salt and freshly ground black pepper
2 (2-pound) lobsters, cooked as for Perfectly Grilled Whole Lobsters (page 127), meat removed and coarsely chopped
8 (6-inch) flour tortillas
1 bunch watercress, coarsely chopped

1. Heat your grill to high.

2. Whisk together the lime juice, chipotle puree, honey, and oil in a medium bowl. Add the tomatoes, mint, and cilantro and season with salt and pepper. Add the lobster meat and mix gently to combine.

3. Grill the tortillas for about 10 seconds per side to warm through and mark slightly.

4. Fill each tortilla with some of the lobster mixture and top with some of the watercress.

Grilled Lobster Rolls with Lemon–Black Pepper Mayonnaise

Lemony lobster salad with a kick of black pepper on a crisp buttered and grilled bun . . . that's nothing but delicious. This lobster salad would also be great served on a mound of mixed greens for a light summer lunch or spooned onto fancy crackers for an elegant passed hors d'oeuvre.

Serves 4 to 8

¾ cup mayonnaise
Grated zest of 1 lemon
Juice of 1 lemon
1 large stalk celery, finely diced
1 small red onion, finely diced
2 tablespoons finely chopped fresh chives
1 tablespoon finely chopped fresh tarragon
    leaves

1 teaspoon coarsely ground black pepper
1 teaspoon kosher salt
Perfectly Grilled Whole Lobsters (page 127),
    meat removed and coarsely chopped
8 hot dog buns, split three quarters of the way
    through
8 tablespoons (1 stick) unsalted butter,
    softened

1. Stir together the mayonnaise, lemon zest and juice, celery, onion, chives, tarragon, pepper, and salt in a large bowl. Add the lobster meat and stir to combine. The lobster salad can be covered and refrigerated for up to 2 hours.

2. Heat your grill to high.

3. Brush the inside of the buns with the butter and place, butter side down, on the grill. Grill until lightly golden brown, 30 to 40 seconds.

4. Divide the lobster salad among the buns and serve immediately.

Grilled Lobster Tails
with White Clam Sauce

Every now and then I get a yearning for a big bowl of perfectly cooked linguine smothered in a garlicky white clam sauce. The sauce, packed with juicy, plump clams, is slightly briny, slightly spicy, and slightly creamy from the olive oil and a little butter added at the end. Though I haven't figured out how to grill pasta just yet, I have figured out that the sauce is equally good, if not better, served over grilled lobster tails. If you aren't able to find fresh chopped clams in your supermarket or fish market, feel free to substitute a high-quality canned version.

Serves 4

3 tablespoons extra-virgin olive oil
3 cloves garlic, finely chopped
1 serrano chile, finely chopped
1 cup dry white wine
1 pound chopped littleneck clams or cockles and their juices
2 teaspoons finely chopped fresh oregano leaves

2 teaspoons honey
1 tablespoon unsalted butter, cold
3 tablespoons finely chopped fresh flat-leaf parsley leaves plus 2 tablespoons whole leaves, for garnish
Kosher salt and freshly ground black pepper
Perfectly Grilled Lobster Tails (page 128)

1. Heat 1 tablespoon of the olive oil in a medium saucepan over high heat. Add the garlic and serrano chile and cook for 30 seconds. Add the wine and boil until reduced by half, about 5 minutes. Add the clams and oregano and cook, stirring occasionally, until the clams are just cooked, 3 to 4 minutes. Stir in the remaining 2 tablespoons olive oil, the honey, butter, and chopped parsley and season with salt and pepper.

2. Remove the lobster tails from the grill, spoon the sauce over them, and garnish with the whole parsley leaves.

mushrooms

Marinated Grilled Portobello Mushrooms • French Bread Pizza with Mushroom Pesto and Fontina Cheese • Stuffed Portobellos with Sausage, Spinach, and Fresh Mozzarella Cheese • Grilled Mushroom and Shaved Celery Heart Salad with Creamy Lemon-Basil Vinaigrette and Parmigiano-Reggiano • Grilled Portobello Mushrooms with Hazelnut Pesto and Goat Cheese • Grilled Shiitake Mushroom Vinaigrette • Grilled Cremini Mushroom, Fontina, and Arugula Pressed Tacos • Shiitake Mushrooms with Spicy Plum-Ginger Glaze

I hold a place in my heart for all mushrooms, from the common white button to the exalted truffle and everything in between. Mushrooms are earthy, woodsy, rich, and meaty. I've seen a grilled portobello mushroom cap satisfy even the most avid meat eater on more than one occasion.

Generally, mushrooms gain depth of flavor as they move across the scale from pale to dark and small to large. The larger, darker, and more open the mushroom is, the more pronounced its flavor is. Conversely, the smaller, paler, and more tightly closed cap the mushroom has, the more delicate it is. Many of the mushroom varieties that you might think of as wild, such as shiitakes and chanterelles, are actually cultivated. Truly wild mushrooms are a rare treat, but of course you need to make sure that you get them from sources who really know their stuff. I use cultivated mushrooms all the time and am always pleased with their quality.

Mushrooms shouldn't be cleaned with water unless they are extremely dirty. A brush or a kitchen towel is best for wiping away any surface grit. Mushrooms become easily water-logged and, in addition, wet mushroom caps quickly become slimy. As for mushroom storage, take them out of plastic and store in a paper bag in the vegetable drawer of your refrigerator. Most will last about a week, but the firmer, drier types such as fresh shiitakes and morels can last up to two weeks.

While raw mushrooms can be nice in a green salad, I almost always prefer them cooked. Grilling is an optimal way to transform mushrooms into something bigger, deeper, and heartier than they ever could be in their raw state. Other methods of cooking mushrooms almost always utilize some sort of liquid or fat; grilling doesn't. So what you end up with is the pure, unadulterated, heat-concentrated flavor of the mushroom and nothing else. Regardless of their final presentation, all sizes of mushrooms can be easily grilled, no special grilling basket needed. If you want them sliced—just do it *after* they come off of the grill! It's a pretty simple answer to a commonly asked question.

Marinated Grilled Portobello Mushrooms

The steps of this dish are somewhat reversed from what one normally thinks of when it comes to marinating: the mushrooms are grilled before they sit in the marinade, not after. The grilled mushrooms absorb a tremendous amount of flavor as they rest. This is an Italian style of preparing vegetables and I like to serve these as a part of an antipasto platter with meats, cheeses, olives, and the like.

Serves 4

¼ cup red wine vinegar
1 tablespoon Dijon mustard
2 cloves garlic, finely chopped
Pinch of red chile flakes
1 tablespoon finely chopped fresh thyme leaves
2 tablespoons finely chopped fresh flat-leaf parsley leaves

½ cup olive oil
Kosher salt and freshly ground black pepper
8 medium portobello mushrooms, stems removed
¼ cup canola oil

1. Heat your grill to medium.

2. Whisk together the vinegar, mustard, garlic, red chile flakes, thyme, and parsley in a medium bowl. Slowly whisk in the olive oil until emulsified. Season with salt and pepper. The marinade can be made 4 hours in advance and refrigerated.

3. Brush both sides of the mushrooms with the canola oil and season with salt and pepper. Place the mushrooms on the grill, cap side down, and grill until golden brown and slightly charred, 4 to 5 minutes. Turn the mushrooms over and continue grilling until just cooked through, 3 to 4 minutes longer.

4. Remove the mushrooms from the grill and cut into ½-inch-thick slices. Place the mushrooms in a large bowl, add the marinade, and toss to coat. Let marinate at room temperature for 30 minutes before serving. The marinated mushrooms can be made 4 hours in advance and refrigerated. Serve cold or at room temperature.

French Bread Pizza with Mushroom Pesto and Fontina Cheese

Classic pesto is an uncooked sauce made of olive oil, basil, pine nuts, and Parmigiano-Reggiano. However, pesto has advanced beyond this traditional preparation and today you can use just about anything to create your own unique version. Mushrooms are a great choice because of their incredible texture and earthy flavor. This isn't your neighborhood pizza parlor's mushroom pizza.

Serves 2 to 4

1 ounce dried porcini mushrooms
1½ pounds cremini or white button mushrooms,
   stems removed
¼ cup canola oil
Kosher salt and freshly ground black pepper
2 cloves roasted garlic (page 38)
¼ cup walnuts, toasted (page 19)
½ cup loosely packed fresh flat-leaf parsley
   leaves, plus more for garnish

2 teaspoons fresh thyme leaves
¾ cup extra-virgin olive oil
¼ cup plus 3 tablespoons grated Pecorino
   Romano cheese
1 loaf French bread or round loaf of bread,
   sliced in half lengthwise
10 ounces fontina cheese, grated (2½ cups)

1. Place the porcini mushrooms in a bowl and cover with boiling water. Let sit until softened, 30 minutes.

2. Heat your grill to high.

3. Brush the cremini mushroom caps with the canola oil and season with salt and pepper. Place the mushrooms on the grill, cap side down, and grill until golden brown and slightly charred, 4 to 5 minutes. Turn the caps over and continue grilling until the mushrooms are cooked through, about 5 minutes longer. Remove from the grill, let cool slightly, and then coarsely chop. Keep the grill on.

4. Remove the porcinis from the soaking liquid and place in the bowl of a food processor with a few tablespoons of the soaking liquid. Add the cremini mushrooms, garlic, walnuts, parsley, and thyme and process until finely chopped. With the motor running, slowly add ½ cup of the olive oil and process until smooth. Add ¼ cup of the Romano cheese and pulse a few times to incorporate. Season with salt and pepper.

5. Brush the bread on the cut side with the remaining ¼ cup olive oil and season with salt and pepper. Place on the grill, oiled side down, and grill until golden brown, about 1 minute.

6. Remove the bread from the grill and evenly spread the pesto over the cut side of each half. Top the pesto with the fontina cheese. Return to the grill, cheese side up; close the cover of the grill; and cook until the cheese has melted, about 2 minutes.

7. Remove from the grill and sprinkle with the remaining 3 tablespoons Romano cheese. Cut each half into 4 equal pieces crosswise, garnish with parsley leaves, and serve.

Stuffed Portobellos with Sausage, Spinach, and Fresh Mozzarella Cheese

You couldn't stop me from ordering this were I to see it on a menu, and to be honest, everyone will have trouble stopping themselves from chowing down these delicious stuffed mushrooms. Italian sausage and fresh mozzarella elevate an often-mundane cocktail-party offering to mythic status. Spinach and fresh herbs keep these meaty portobello caps fresh, while red chile flakes and garlic add a nice touch of heat. You could serve these whole as a hearty first course, pair them with a simple salad for a satisfying meal, or cut them into wedges and serve as an appetizer or a side dish.

Serves 4

6 tablespoons olive oil
12 ounces mild Italian sausage, casings removed
1 medium Spanish onion, finely chopped
2 cloves garlic, finely chopped
¼ teaspoon red chile flakes
½ cup dry red wine
8 ounces fresh spinach leaves, stems removed, coarsely chopped
Kosher salt and freshly ground black pepper

2 tablespoons chopped fresh basil leaves, plus more for garnish
2 tablespoons chopped fresh flat-leaf parsley leaves, plus more for garnish
12 ounces fresh mozzarella, cut into small cubes
4 large portobello mushrooms, stems removed
2 plum tomatoes, thinly sliced

1. Heat 2 tablespoons of the oil in a large sauté pan over high heat. Add the sausage and, using a wooden spoon, break it up into small pieces. Cook until golden brown and cooked through, about 5 minutes. Remove the sausage with a slotted spoon to a plate lined with paper towels.

2. Add the onion to the pan and cook until soft, 3 to 4 minutes. Add the garlic and red chile flakes and cook for 30 seconds. Return the sausage to the pan, add the wine, and simmer until the wine has completely evaporated. Add the spinach and ½ cup water and season with salt and pepper. Cook until the spinach has wilted, about 2 minutes. Remove from the heat and stir in the basil, parsley, and mozzarella and let cool slightly.

3. Heat your grill to high.

4. Brush the mushrooms caps on both sides with the remaining 4 tablespoons oil and season with salt and pepper. Place the mushrooms on the grill, oiled side down, and cook until golden brown, about 4 minutes.

5. Remove the mushrooms from the grill and place on a flat surface, cap side down. Fill the mushrooms with the sausage mixture and top each with a few slices of tomato. Season the tomatoes with salt and pepper and place the mushrooms on the grill, cap side down. Close the cover and cook until the mushrooms and filling have heated through, the cheese has melted, and the tomatoes are soft, about 5 minutes.

6. Remove to a platter and sprinkle with the basil and parsley, if desired.

Grilled Mushroom Heart Salad with Creamy Lemon-Basil Vinaigrette and Parmigiano-Reggiano

I think celery is an under-utilized vegetable. Sometimes I find myself using it only as an aromatic to flavor soups and sauces until I remember how great it is eaten raw. The crisp texture and slightly bitter flavor are a perfect complement to the meaty texture of mushrooms. The same thing goes for parsley in that it is too often used just as a garnish. Italian flat-leaf parsley has tons of flavor and the whole leaves are a great addition to salads.

Serves 4 to 6

1 pound cremini or white button mushrooms,
    stems trimmed
3 tablespoons canola oil
Kosher salt and freshly ground black pepper
2 stalks celery (the white stalks from the heart),
    thinly sliced

4 ounces mesclun greens
¼ cup fresh flat-leaf parsley leaves
Creamy Lemon-Basil Vinaigrette
    (recipe follows)
2 ounces Parmigiano-Reggiano, thinly shaved
    with a vegetable peeler

1. Heat your grill to high.

2. Place the mushrooms in a large bowl. Add the canola oil, season with salt and pepper, and toss to coat. Place the mushrooms on the grill, cap side down, and grill until golden brown and slightly charred, 4 to 5 minutes. Turn over and continue grilling until just cooked through, 3 to 4 minutes longer. Remove from the grill and cut into ⅛-inch-thick slices.

3. Put the celery, mesclun greens, and parsley in a large bowl; add half of the vinaigrette and toss to combine. Season with salt and pepper. Top with the mushrooms and drizzle with more of the vinaigrette. Top with the shaved Parmigiano-Reggiano and additional pepper.

Creamy Lemon-Basil Vinaigrette

Makes ⅔ cup

Grated zest of 1 lemon
¼ cup fresh lemon juice
2 tablespoons mayonnaise
1 teaspoon honey

½ teaspoon kosher salt
¼ teaspoon freshly ground black pepper
¼ cup fresh basil leaves
½ cup extra-virgin olive oil

Combine the lemon zest, juice, mayonnaise, honey, salt, pepper, basil, and olive oil in a blender and blend until smooth. The vinaigrette can be made 1 hour in advance and refrigerated.

Grilled Portobello Mushrooms with Hazelnut Pesto and Goat Cheese

If you are looking for a great vegetarian entrée, it doesn't get much better than this. Portobello mushrooms are rich, hearty, and almost beefy in flavor, and the hazelnut pesto not only is delicious, but it also brings some natural protein to the dish. That all being said, I am definitely not a vegetarian and I love this dish as a side or starter. The creamy, tangy goat cheese will melt a bit from the heat of the mushrooms, making each bite a heavenly one.

Serves 4

4 large portobello mushrooms, stems removed
3 tablespoons canola oil
Kosher salt and freshly ground black pepper
Hazelnut Pesto (recipe follows)

6 ounces fresh goat cheese, cut into small pieces
Fresh flat-leaf parsley leaves, for garnish
Fresh basil leaves, for garnish
2 teaspoons grated lemon zest

1. Heat your grill to high.

2. Brush the mushrooms on both sides with the oil and season with salt and pepper. Place the mushrooms on the grill, cap side down, and grill until golden brown and slightly charred, 4 to 5 minutes. Turn the mushrooms over and continue grilling until just cooked through, 3 to 4 minutes.

3. Transfer the mushrooms to a platter, cap side down, and top with a few tablespoons of the hazelnut pesto and some of the goat cheese. Garnish with parsley leaves, basil leaves, and lemon zest.

Hazelnut Pesto

Makes about ¾ cup

1½ cups fresh flat-leaf parsley leaves
8 fresh basil leaves
½ cup hazelnuts
2 cloves garlic
¼ cup plus 2 tablespoons extra-virgin olive oil

1 tablespoon hazelnut oil, optional
3 tablespoons freshly grated
   Parmigiano-Reggiano
Kosher salt and freshly ground black pepper

Combine the parsley, basil, hazelnuts, garlic, olive and hazelnut oils, cheese, and salt and pepper to taste in a food processor and process until smooth. The pesto can be made 2 hours in advance, covered, and refrigerated. Bring to room temperature before serving.

Grilled Shiitake Mushroom Vinaigrette

This amazing vinaigrette is not really meant for green salads but as a delicious sauce for meat, poultry, and fish, such as salmon. It's also perfect spread on grilled bread for a quick and easy appetizer. Actually, the chewy texture of the shiitakes with the sweet flavor of the shallots and balsamic vinegar is so good that you might find yourself digging into this with a spoon. Feel free to add a tablespoon of any other fresh herb in addition to the parsley. Rosemary would be wonderful with grilled beef, sage with chicken, and thyme with grilled fish. Also, button, cremini, and portobello mushrooms would all work well in this vinaigrette, so use one or all of them in addition to the shiitake mushrooms should you prefer.

Makes 4 cups

4 large shiitake mushrooms, stems removed
3 tablespoons canola oil
Kosher salt and freshly ground black pepper
2 shallots, finely diced
3 tablespoons balsamic vinegar

2 teaspoons Dijon mustard
½ cup extra-virgin olive oil
3 tablespoons finely chopped fresh flat-leaf
   parsley leaves

1. Heat your grill to high.

2. Brush both sides of the mushroom caps with the canola oil and season with salt and pepper. Place on the grill, cap side down, and grill until golden brown and slightly charred, 4 to 5 minutes. Turn the mushrooms over and continue cooking until just cooked through, 3 to 4 minutes longer. Remove from the grill and coarsely chop.

3. Whisk together the shallots, vinegar, mustard, olive oil, and parsley in a medium bowl until combined. Season with salt and pepper. Add the mushrooms and stir to coat. Let sit at room temperature for at least 15 minutes or up to 1 hour before serving. The vinaigrette can be made 1 day in advance, covered, and refrigerated. Bring to room temperature before serving.

Grilled Cremini Mushroom, Fontina, and Arugula Pressed Tacos

You could also think of these as southwestern panini or as Italian quesadillas. Regardless of what you call them, these pressed tacos taste incredible. Rich, garlicky mushrooms and peppery arugula fused together with nutty fontina cheese between crispy tortillas make for a sensational treat. These tacos make great appetizers in smaller portions and also work well for lunch when served with a green salad.

Serves 4 to 8

¾ pound cremini mushrooms, stems removed
6 tablespoons canola oil
1 tablespoon chopped fresh thyme leaves
2 cloves garlic, finely chopped
Kosher salt and freshly ground black pepper

8 (6-inch) flour tortillas
¾ pound fontina cheese, coarsely grated (3 cups)
1 red onion, halved and thinly sliced
3 ounces baby arugula leaves

1. Place the mushroom caps in a bowl; add 3 tablespoons of the oil, the thyme, and garlic, and toss to combine. Let sit at room temperature for at least 15 minutes and up to 1 hour.

2. Heat your grill to high.

3. Season the mushrooms with salt and pepper and place on the grill, cap side down. Grill until golden brown and slightly charred, 4 to 5 minutes. Turn over and continue grilling until the mushrooms are soft and just cooked through, 3 to 4 minutes longer. Remove from the grill, let cool slightly, and then thinly slice.

4. Lay the tortillas on a flat surface and place some of the cheese on one side of the tortilla. Top the cheese with some of the mushrooms, the onions, and several arugula leaves. Place a little more of the cheese over the arugula and fold to make half moons.

5. Brush the tops of the tortillas with some of the remaining oil and place on the grill, oiled side down. Grill until golden brown and crisp, 2 to 3 minutes. Brush the tortillas with the remaining oil, flip them over, and continue grilling until golden brown and the cheese has melted, 1 to 2 minutes longer. Cut into wedges before serving, if desired.

Shiitake Mushrooms with Spicy Plum-Ginger Glaze

Asian flavors really make this glaze unique. Store any leftover glaze in the refrigerator and use it the next day on chicken, duck, or lamb.

Serves 4 to 6

6 tablespoons canola oil
3 shallots, fincly chopped
2 Thai chiles, seeded and finely chopped
3 cloves garlic, finely chopped
3 tablespoons finely chopped peeled fresh ginger
2 tablespoons mild curry powder
1 teaspoon ground cinnamon
2 star anise

6 purple plums, pitted and coarsely chopped
2 tablespoons soy sauce
¼ cup light brown sugar
2 tablespoons honey
Kosher salt and freshly ground black pepper
12 medium shiitake mushrooms, stems removed
3 tablespoons finely chopped fresh chives

1. Heat 3 tablespoons of the oil in a large nonreactive saucepan over medium-high heat. Add the shallots and cook until soft, 2 to 3 minutes. Add the Thai chiles, garlic, and ginger, and cook for 1 minute. Add the curry powder and cinnamon and cook for 2 minutes. Add the star anise, plums, soy sauce, brown sugar, honey, and 1 cup water and cook, stirring occasionally, until the plums become very soft and the sauce thickens, 20 to 30 minutes. Remove from the heat and let cool slightly.

2. Transfer the plum mixture to a food processor, season with salt and pepper, and process until smooth. Strain into a bowl and let cool to room temperature.

3. Heat your grill to high.

4. Brush the mushrooms on both sides with the remaining 3 tablespoons oil and season with salt and pepper. Place the mushrooms on the grill, cap side down, and grill until golden brown, 3 to 4 minutes. Turn over and brush with the plum glaze. Continue grilling and brushing with the glaze until the mushrooms are just cooked through, about 5 minutes longer.

5. Transfer to a platter and sprinkle with the chives.

pork

Marinated Pork Chops with Blood Orange and Rosemary • Blue Corn Cuban Taco • Basil-Rubbed Pork Chops with Nectarine–Blue Cheese Salad and Toasted Pine Nuts • Grilled Sausage Sandwiches with Onion Sauce and Grilled Pepper Relish • Smoked Paprika–Rubbed Pork Tenderloin Sandwich with Grilled Red Onion and Sage Aioli • Maple-Peach Glazed Pork Tenderloin • Molasses-Mustard Glazed Pork Chops with Apple Butter • Grilled Pork Chops with Port Wine Vinaigrette, Grilled Figs, and Walnut Oil • Pork Gyros with Yogurt-Tomato Sauce, Red Onion, and Spinach

Many people tend to think of pork as a fatty, unhealthy choice. Maybe that's because so many of us would name bacon as our favorite form of pork? Whatever the reason, it's simply not true. The pork raised in this country today is leaner and healthier than ever before with meat that is predominately tender and delicately flavored. So it's good for you (bacon aside), generally inexpensive, always available . . . and delicious! If you grew up on pork chops broiled so dry that no amount of applesauce could ease them down your throat and have been holding a grudge against them ever since, you might want to give pork another shot.

One factor for the dry pork of our youth was the fear of trichinosis, a parasite killed at high temperatures. While I wouldn't go so far as to say that it has been eradicated, today's pork can be safely cooked to a lower internal temperature. (The very young, very old, people with compromised immune systems, and pregnant women should, however, continue to have their pork cooked according to the FDA guidelines.) Pork served at medium doneness will be incomparably more juicy than that cooked to well done. Pork today just doesn't have enough fat to remain juicy past medium, so unless you like chewing for hours on one bite, don't overcook your pork. And remember, the pork will continue to cook—coming up in temperature as many as 10 degrees when resting, so allow for that when calculating doneness.

Like beef tenderloin, pork tenderloin is soft and mild in flavor. I love to pair it with rubs to create a crusty, dynamic texture and add tons of flavor. That's one of the biggest reasons that grilling is my cooking method of choice when cooking pork. Even without the added bonus of a rub, the grill's direct heat transforms pork by giving it a beautifully charred and crusty exterior. Cooked properly (a.k.a. not for too long!), the inside will stay tender and succulent while the outside garners a gorgeous crust. Grilling instantly adds its distinct flavor *and* additional texture to pork—why would you want to cook it any other way?

Marinated Pork Chops
Blood Orange and Rosemary

This marinade is Sicilian in inspiration; they love their blood oranges and rosemary in Sicily! It's a somewhat unexpected, totally delicious combination that gives real zest to otherwise mild pork chops. Blood oranges not only are gorgeous in color, but they also have a slightly sour tang that navel oranges lack. Balsamic vinegar, with its own play of sweet and tangy, is a great match for the blood orange juice. Robust rosemary adds a pop of fresh pine-like flavor to the marinade and keeps the whole dish grounded with an overall savory, not sweet, taste. If blood orange juice isn't available or out-of-season use two parts orange juice to one part cranberry juice.

Serves 4

2½ cups fresh blood orange juice (from 8 to 10 large blood oranges)
½ cup olive oil
2 tablespoons balsamic vinegar
2 tablespoons chopped fresh rosemary leaves

4 (1-inch-thick) center-cut bone-in pork loin chops
1 tablespoon honey
Kosher salt and freshly ground black pepper

1. Whisk together ½ cup of the juice, ¼ cup of the oil, 1 tablespoon of the vinegar, and the rosemary in a large baking dish. Add the pork chops and turn to coat in the marinade. Cover and refrigerate for at least 1 hour and up to 4 hours.

2. Pour the remaining 2 cups juice into a small saucepan and boil over high heat until reduced to 3 tablespoons. Transfer the reduced juice to a blender, add the remaining 1 tablespoon vinegar and the honey, and blend until smooth. With the motor running, slowly add the remaining ¼ cup oil and blend until emulsified. Season with salt and pepper. The vinaigrette can be made 4 hours in advance and refrigerated. Bring to room temperature before serving.

3. Heat your grill to medium-high.

4. Remove the pork from the marinade and season with salt and pepper on both sides. Grill for 4 to 5 minutes per side until golden brown and slightly charred.

5. Remove from the grill and immediately drizzle with the vinaigrette. Tent loosely with foil and let rest for 5 minutes before slicing ½ inch thick.

Blue Corn Cuban Taco

Cuban sandwiches are one of my favorite things to eat, so I had to figure out a way to serve them at my southwestern restaurant Mesa Grill. This is what I came up with. While the classic Cuban sandwich is made with pork shoulder that has been braised for several hours in a stock flavored with citrus, garlic, and herbs, I opted for a quicker version made with fast-cooking pork tenderloin. I marinate the pork to get that garlicky kick and then grill it until slightly charred for additional flavor and texture. To keep things southwestern, blue corn tortillas replace the soft and sweet Cuban bread, and spicy pickled jalapeños replace the pickles.

Serves 4

6 tablespoons canola oil
Juice of 1 orange
3 cloves garlic, chopped
2 tablespoons chopped fresh oregano leaves
1½ pounds pork tenderloin, fat trimmed
8 (6-inch) blue corn tortillas

8 thin slices Swiss cheese, sliced in half
8 thin slices smoked ham
4 pickled jalapeño chiles, drained and thinly sliced
Grilled Red Pepper Relish (page 163), optional
Fresh cilantro leaves, for garnish, optional

1. Whisk together 3 tablespoons of the oil, the orange juice, garlic, and oregano in a baking dish. Add the pork and turn to coat. Cover and marinate in the refrigerator for at least 1 hour and up to 4 hours.

2. Heat your grill to high.

3. Remove the pork from the marinade and place on the grill. Grill until golden brown and slightly charred and an instant-read thermometer inserted into the center of the meat registers 150 degrees F, 12 to 15 minutes. Remove from the grill, tent loosely with foil, and let rest for 5 minutes before slicing into ¼-inch-thick slices.

4. Reduce the heat of the grill to medium. Place the tortillas on the grill and grill for approximately 10 seconds per side to make them pliable. Lay the tortillas on a flat surface. Divide the ingredients evenly over one half of each tortilla. Start with 1 slice of the cheese, followed by a slice of the ham, then a few slices of the pork, a few slices of the jalapeños, and another slice of the cheese. Fold the tops of the tortillas over the ingredients and press on them.

5. Brush the tops of the tortillas with some of the remaining oil and place on the grill, oiled side down. Grill until lightly golden brown, pressing on each tortilla to flatten it, 3 to 4 minutes. Brush the tops of the tortillas with the remaining oil, flip them over, and continue grilling, pressing down on the tortillas until golden brown and the cheese has melted.

6. Cut into wedges and top each wedge with a dollop of the relish and some cilantro leaves, if desired, before serving.

Basil-Rubbed Pork Chops with Nectarine–Blue Cheese Salad and Toasted Pine Nuts

Rubbing pork chops with leaves of basil is a great way to imbue the chops with the essential oils and taste of sweet basil without grilling the actual herb, which would burn and turn bitter on the grill. Fruit and pork are a famous combination (pork chops and applesauce, anyone?), and these grilled nectarines are a delicious summer twist. Blue cheese—so good with grilled peaches and nectarines—adds a nice, salty kick. Toasted pine nuts are there as much for their light crunch factor as they are for their buttery taste. A garnish of basil ribbons ties everything together.

Serves 4

4 (1-inch-thick) center-cut boneless pork chops
16 basil leaves: 8 left whole and 8 sliced into ribbons
4 tablespoons olive oil
Kosher salt and freshly ground black pepper

4 nectarines, slightly underripe, halved and pitted
4 ounces blue cheese, crumbled (1 cup)
2 tablespoons honey
¼ cup pine nuts, toasted (see page 19)
Coarsely ground black pepper

1. Heat your grill to high.

2. Rub each side of the pork chops with a basil leaf, brush with 2 tablespoons of the oil, and season with salt and pepper. Grill for 4 to 5 minutes per side or until slightly charred and just cooked through. Remove to a plate, tent loosely with foil, and let rest for 5 minutes.

3. While the pork is resting, brush the cut side of the nectarines with the remaining 2 tablespoons oil and place on the grill, cut side down. Grill for 2 to 3 minutes or until golden brown and caramelized. Turn over and grill for 1 to 2 minutes or until slightly soft.

4. Remove the nectarines from the grill and top each half with some blue cheese. Drizzle with honey and garnish with the basil ribbons, pine nuts, and a sprinkling of the black pepper. Serve alongside the pork chops.

Grilled Sausage Sandwiches with Onion Sauce and Grilled Pepper Relish

I think of this sandwich as Little Italy meets New York hot-dog vendor. I am not really sure what the genesis of the onion sauce is, but you can find it on every hot-dog cart in New York City and I love it. And, of course, no visit to Little Italy is complete without sausage and peppers.

Serves 4

Grilled Red Pepper Relish

3 red bell peppers, grilled (see page 120), peeled, seeded, and coarsely chopped
3 cloves roasted garlic (page 38), coarsely chopped
2 tablespoons red wine vinegar
3 tablespoons extra-virgin olive oil
2 tablespoons finely chopped fresh flat-leaf parsley leaves
2 tablespoons finely chopped fresh basil leaves
Kosher salt and freshly ground black pepper

Grilled Italian Sausage

4 hot or sweet Italian sausage links
4 tablespoons olive oil
Kosher salt and freshly ground black pepper
4 hoagie buns, split three-quarters of the way through
¼ cup Dijon mustard
Onion Sauce (recipe follows)

1. Heat your grill to medium-high.

2. Combine the peppers, garlic, red wine vinegar, extra-virgin olive oil, parsley, and basil in a medium bowl and season with salt and pepper. Let the relish sit at room temperature for 30 minutes before serving.

3. Brush the sausages with 2 tablespoons of the olive oil and season with salt and pepper. Grill the sausages until golden brown, slightly charred on all sides, and cooked through, about 12 to 15 minutes.

4. Brush the inside of the buns with the remaining 2 tablespoons olive oil and season with salt and pepper. Place on the grill, cut side down, and grill until lightly golden brown, about 1 minute.

5. Spread the bottom half of each bun with some of the mustard and top with a sausage and some of the onion sauce and grilled pepper relish.

Onion Sauce

Makes approximately ¾ cup

2 tablespoons canola oil
2 large onions, halved and cut ¼ inch thick
1 teaspoon ancho chile powder
½ teaspoon ground cinnamon

¼ cup ketchup
1 teaspoon hot sauce
½ teaspoon kosher salt
¼ teaspoon freshly ground black pepper

1. Heat the oil in a medium saucepan over medium heat. Add the onions, and cook, stirring occasionally, until soft, about 10 minutes. Stir in the chile powder and cinnamon and cook for 1 minute.

2. Add the ketchup, ½ cup water, the hot sauce, salt, and black pepper and bring to a simmer. Cook for 10 to 15 minutes or until thickened. Transfer to a bowl and let cool to room temperature. The onion sauce can be made 1 day in advance, covered, and refrigerated. Bring to room temperature before serving.

Smoked Paprika–Rubbed Pork Tenderloin Sandwich with Grilled Red Onion and Sage Aioli

I find that most home cooks tend to use sage only once a year in their Thanksgiving stuffing. And even then, most of them use the dried variety, which tastes nothing like the fresh. Fresh sage has a very pungent, almost balsam-like flavor and should be used with a light hand, as a little goes a long way. If fresh sage isn't available or you just don't enjoy the taste, you can easily substitute fresh basil in the aioli. Smoked Spanish paprika has a much deeper flavor than the variety that you will find in your supermarket spice aisle. I have been using it for years at my Spanish restaurant Bolo and find its flavor unparalleled. It's available in specialty food markets or online.

Serves 4

¼ cup canola oil
2 tablespoons smoked Spanish paprika
1 tablespoon kosher salt
1½ pounds pork tenderloin, trimmed of fat
Sage Aioli (recipe follows)

4 crusty rolls, split three-quarters of the way through
1 large red onion, cut into ½-inch-thick slices, grilled (see page 120), and separated into rings
1 cup packed baby arugula

1. Heat your grill to high.

2. Whisk together the oil, paprika, and salt in a small bowl. Rub the tenderloin with the mixture and let sit for 5 minutes.

3. Place the pork on the grill and cook until golden brown and slightly charred on all sides and an instant-read thermometer inserted into the center registers 150 degrees F, 12 to 15 minutes. Remove from the grill, tent loosely with foil, and let rest for 5 minutes before slicing into ½-inch-thick slices.

4. Spread some of the sage aioli on the bottom and top half of each roll. Top the bottom half with several pieces of the pork, then some onion, and finally some arugula.

Sage Aioli

Makes ½ cup

½ cup mayonnaise
2 cloves garlic
2 tablespoons chopped fresh sage leaves

2 teaspoons fresh lemon juice
Kosher salt and freshly ground black pepper

Combine the mayonnaise, garlic, sage, lemon juice, and salt and pepper to taste in a food processor and process until smooth. Transfer to a bowl and refrigerate for at least 30 minutes or up to 8 hours before serving.

Maple-Peach Glazed Pork Tenderloin

This glaze couldn't be easier to throw together from items that you most likely already have on hand in your pantry and refrigerator. Combine that with a quick-cooking pork tenderloin, and you've got an easy dinner entrée for any night of the week. Maple syrup, orange juice, and peach preserves are balanced with fresh thyme and a touch of heat. See photograph on page 154.

Serves 4

¾ cup peach preserves
3 tablespoons pure maple syrup
3 tablespoons orange juice (not from concentrate)
1 tablespoon ancho chile powder
2 teaspoons finely chopped fresh thyme
   leaves, plus whole sprigs for garnish

Kosher salt and freshly ground black pepper
1½ pounds pork tenderloin
2 tablespoons canola oil
Thai red chile, thinly sliced (optional)

1. Whisk together the preserves, syrup, juice, ancho powder, thyme, and salt and pepper to taste in a small bowl. Let sit for 15 minutes before using.

2. Heat your grill to high.

3. Brush the tenderloin with the oil and season with salt and pepper. Grill until golden brown and slightly charred on all sides and an instant-read thermometer inserted into the center registers 150 degrees F, 12 to 15 minutes. Brush with some of the peach glaze during the last 5 minutes of grilling.

4. Remove from the grill and brush with the remaining glaze. Tent loosely with foil and let rest for 2 minutes before slicing into ½-inch-thick slices. Garnish with the sliced chile and thyme sprigs.

Molasses-Mustard Glazed Pork Chops with Apple Butter

I serve these pork chops at my restaurant Bar Americain, where they consistently sell out every night. Apple butter is a more sophisticated spin on the old standby applesauce and is—while still sweet—rich and savory. Granny Smiths are the best apples to use here due to their slightly tart, not-too-sweet taste. Deep, dark molasses makes for a beautifully glazed chop. Mustard—and I use a combination of sharp Dijon for flavor and whole-grain mustard for looks and texture—has an appealing tanginess that keeps the sweet molasses from being overpowering.

Serves 4

¼ cup Dijon mustard
2 tablespoons whole-grain mustard
¼ cup molasses
Kosher salt and freshly ground black pepper

4 (1-inch-thick) bone-in center-cut pork chops
2 tablespoons canola oil
Apple Butter (recipe follows)

1. Whisk together both mustards, the molasses, and salt and pepper to taste in a small bowl.

2. Heat the grill to high.

3. Brush the chops on both sides with the oil and season with salt and pepper. Place on the grill and grill until golden brown and slightly charred, 3 to 4 minutes. Brush the chops with the glaze, turn over, and continue grilling to medium, 4 to 5 minutes. Brush with more of the glaze during the last minute of cooking. Remove the chops from the grill, tent loosely with foil, and let rest for 5 minutes. Top each with a dollop of the apple butter.

Apple Butter

Makes approximately 1 cup

2 tablespoons canola oil

1 small Spanish onion, finely chopped

1 clove garlic, finely chopped

2 large Granny Smith apples, peeled, cored, and chopped

3 tablespoons light brown sugar

1 teaspoon ground cinnamon

¼ teaspoon kosher salt

12 tablespoons (1½ sticks) unsalted butter, softened

1. Heat the oil in a large sauté pan over medium-high heat. Add the onion and cook until soft, 3 to 4 minutes. Add the garlic and cook for 30 seconds longer. Add the apples and brown sugar and cook until the apples are very soft but still retain some of their shape, 5 to 7 minutes.

2. Stir in the cinnamon and salt and cook for 1 minute. Remove the mixture from the heat and let cool.

3. Transfer the mixture to a food processor along with the butter and process until smooth. Scrape into a small bowl, cover, and refrigerate for at least 1 hour or up to 1 day to allow the flavors to meld. Let come to room temperature before serving.

Grilled Pork Chops with Port Wine Vinaigrette, Grilled Figs, and Walnut Oil

This is a totally luscious, borderline decadent preparation for anything-but-ordinary pork chops. Delicate and sweet fresh figs gain extra sweetness from the caramelizing heat of the grill and become a tremendous sauce. Lemony thyme keeps it all fresh-tasting, never cloying. The port wine vinaigrette is rich, complex, and nearly (and deliciously) syrupy in taste and texture due to the addition of molasses and the flavor-packed reduction of port and red wines.

Serves 4

12 fresh figs
4 tablespoons olive oil
2 tablespoons balsamic vinegar
2 tablespoons extra-virgin olive oil

2 teaspoons finely chopped fresh thyme
  leaves
4 (1-inch-thick) boneless pork chops
Kosher salt and freshly ground black pepper
Port Wine Vinaigrette (recipe follows)

1. Heat your grill to high.

2. Brush the figs with 2 tablespoons of the olive oil and grill until golden brown on both sides, 2 to 3 minutes per side. Remove from the grill, let cool slightly, and cut each fig into quarters.

3. Whisk together the vinegar, extra-virgin olive oil, and thyme in a large bowl. Add the figs and gently mix to combine. The fig mixture can be made 30 minutes in advance and kept at room temperature.

4. Brush the chops on both sides with the remaining 2 tablespoons olive oil and season with salt and pepper. Place on the grill and cook until golden brown and slightly charred, 3 to 4 minutes. Turn the chops over, close the cover, and continue cooking until an instant-read thermometer inserted into the center of each chop registers 150 degrees F. Remove from the grill and drizzle with some of the vinaigrette. Tent loosely with foil and let rest for 5 minutes before serving.

5. Serve each chop on a large plate, topped with some of the fig mixture and drizzled with additional vinaigrette.

Port Wine Vinaigrette

Makes approximately ¾ cup

2 tablespoons olive oil
½ small red onion, finely chopped
2 cups port
½ cup dry red wine
1 tablespoon molasses
1 tablespoon honey

3 tablespoons balsamic vinegar
2 teaspoons chopped fresh thyme leaves
½ teaspoon kosher salt
¼ teaspoon ground black pepper
½ cup extra-virgin olive oil
1 tablespoon walnut oil

1. Heat the olive oil in a medium saucepan over high heat. Add the onion and cook until soft, 3 to 4 minutes. Add the port and red wine and boil until thickened and reduced to ½ cup, about 15 minutes.

2. Transfer the reduced wine to a blender and add the molasses, honey, balsamic vinegar, thyme, salt, and pepper and blend until combined. With the motor running, slowly add the extra-virgin olive oil and walnut oil and blend until emulsified. The vinaigrette can be made 1 day in advance, covered, and refrigerated. Bring to room temperature before using.

PORK

169

Pork Gyros with Yogurt-Tomato Sauce, Red Onion, and Spinach

Greek gyros are traditionally filled with meat (pork or lamb mixtures) that has been sliced and stacked onto an upright rotisserie where it cooks, continually basting itself. This tender meat is then shaved off into thin slices that are rolled into a grilled pita with a garlicky yogurt sauce. Sounds delicious, right? Well, it is—so much so that I wanted to make a home kitchen–friendly version. Grilled pork tenderloin marinated in Greek flavors fills the bill. I added some color to the traditional sauce with diced tomato; capers add a nice briny note. I like to serve this gyro with tender baby spinach instead of lettuce for a little extra flavor and with sweet red onions for crunch.

Serves 4

¼ cup olive oil

¼ cup dry red wine

4 cloves garlic, chopped

1 tablespoon finely chopped fresh oregano leaves

2 pounds pork tenderloin

Kosher salt and freshly ground black pepper

4 pita pockets

1½ cups baby spinach

½ red onion, thinly sliced

Yogurt-Tomato Sauce (recipe follows)

1 plum tomato, seeded and diced

1. Whisk together the oil, wine, garlic, and oregano in a baking dish. Add the pork and turn to coat. Cover and marinate in the refrigerator for at least 1 hour and up to 4 hours.

2. Heat your grill to high.

3. Remove the pork from the marinade and pat dry with paper towels and season with salt and pepper. Grill until golden brown on all sides and cooked to an internal temperature of 150 degrees F, 15 to 18 minutes. Transfer to a cutting board, tent loosely with foil, and let rest for 5 minutes before slicing into ¼-inch-thick slices.

4. While the pork is resting, grill the pita pockets for about 10 seconds per side. Transfer to a cutting board and slice off the top inch of each pita.

5. Fill each pita with sliced pork, some spinach and onion, a few spoonfuls of yogurt-tomato sauce, and a sprinkling of diced tomato.

Yogurt-Tomato Sauce

Makes approximately 1½ cups

1 pint Greek yogurt

2 cloves garlic, finely chopped

¼ cup finely grated peeled cucumber

1 plum tomato, seeded and finely diced

2 tablespoons capers, drained

2 tablespoons finely chopped fresh dill

1 tablespoon red wine vinegar

Kosher salt and freshly ground black pepper

Stir together the yogurt, garlic, cucumber, tomato, capers, dill, vinegar, and salt and pepper to taste in a medium bowl. Cover and let sit in the refrigerator for at least 30 minutes and up to 4 hours before serving.

potatoes

French-Style Grilled Potato Salad • "Old Bay" Grilled Steak Fries • Grilled New Potatoes and Zucchini with Radicchio, Goat Cheese, and Aged Sherry Vinaigrette • Grilled Potatoes with Spicy Tomato Mayonnaise • Grilled Potato and Goat Cheese Napoleon with Balsamic-Basil Vinaigrette • Grilled New Potato Salad with Bacon and Buttermilk Dressing • Vinegar and Salt Grilled Potato "Chips" • Grilled Sweet Potato Wedges with Spicy Cranberry-Bourbon Glaze

Grilling might not be the first cooking method you think of when you're hungry for potatoes, but you'd be surprised at how well the two take to each other. There's no reason that the potato shouldn't get its fair share of smoky taste and gorgeous grill marks. Beyond that, there's also something incredibly satisfying about being able to offer a complete meal from the grill—you know, your standard meat and potatoes. A quick parboil is all you'll need to do inside before taking everything you've got out to the grill.

There are tons of potatoes out there and I find a use for just about all of them. I love the gorgeous yellow flesh of Yukon Golds, the tender flesh of baby red bliss potatoes, and the funky shapes of fingerlings; and for beautifully starchy potato-ness, it's hard to beat an Idaho russet. The different types of potatoes have varied growing seasons, so be on the lookout for local varieties. Russets and Yukon Golds are available year-round, thin-skinned new potatoes are in season from late winter through mid-summer, the red bliss take over mid-summer through fall, and fingerlings are available from October through April.

Another year-round favorite is the sweet potato. They are packed with nutrients and are incredibly delicious. They're one of my kitchen staples as I love how their natural sweetness contrasts with so many of the smoky and slightly spicy flavors that I use. I substitute sweet potatoes in potato preparations all the time; feel free to do the same with the recipes here.

All potatoes should be firm and relatively smooth and even in color. Look for ones that are free of eyes and blemishes and have no green tint, soft spots, or sprouts. Potatoes should be stored in a cool and dry area. The refrigerator is not recommended because the super-low temperature converts the potatoes' starch to sugar, which changes their texture.

French-Style Grilled Potato Salad

This potato salad is mayonnaise-free so it's perfect for a picnic. In fact, I actually recommend that you serve it warm or at room temperature and not chilled. The use of red and yellow potatoes is purely aesthetic, so feel free to use just one or the other if you'd like. Chervil is used a lot in French cooking, and to me, it tastes like a lightly anise-flavored parsley. If you can't find chervil, substituting equal parts tarragon and flat-leaf parsley will produce a comparable flavor.

Serves 4

2½ pounds small new potatoes, preferably a mix of red and yellow, scrubbed
Kosher salt
½ cup olive oil
Freshly ground black pepper
¼ cup white wine vinegar

1 tablespoon Dijon mustard
1 clove garlic, finely chopped
1 small red onion, halved and thinly sliced
6 cornichons, finely diced
2 tablespoons capers, drained
¼ cup coarsely chopped fresh chervil leaves

1. Put the potatoes in a pot of salted cold water and bring to a boil. Reduce the heat and simmer until tender, about 8 minutes. Drain and let cool slightly before slicing in half.

2. Heat your grill to medium.

3. Brush the potatoes with ¼ cup of the oil and season with salt and pepper. Place the potatoes on the grill, cut side down, and grill until lightly golden brown, about 4 minutes. Turn the potatoes over and continue grilling until just cooked through, about 4 minutes longer.

4. While the potatoes are grilling, whisk together the vinegar, mustard, and the remaining ¼ cup oil in a large bowl. Add the garlic, red onion, cornichons, and capers, season with salt and pepper, and stir to combine.

5. Remove the potatoes from the grill, immediately add to the bowl with the other ingredients, and gently stir to combine. Season with salt and pepper. Let sit at room temperature for at least 15 minutes and up to 1 hour. Stir in the chervil before serving.

"Old Bay" Grilled Steak Fries

Old Bay is a spice blend originally used in the Chesapeake Bay area and made famous for its use in shrimp, crab, and other seafood dishes. It may be traditionally used in seafood dishes, but I like to play with that notion a little bit and use it to spice up a side dish and these steak fries certainly fit the bill. While the actual recipe for Old Bay is a carefully guarded secret, this homemade spice mixture has all of those favorite flavors: celery, mustard, bay leaf, and ginger. Serve these with Grilled Lobster Rolls with Lemon–Black Pepper Mayonnaise (page 135) or Perfectly Grilled Whole Lobsters (page 127).

Serves 4

1 tablespoon ground bay leaves
2½ teaspoons celery salt
1½ teaspoons dry mustard
1 teaspoon sweet Spanish paprika
1 teaspoon ground black pepper
½ teaspoon ground white pepper
½ teaspoon ground nutmeg
½ teaspoon ground cloves
¼ teaspoon ground allspice

¼ teaspoon ground ginger
¼ teaspoon crushed red chile flakes
¼ teaspoon ground cardamom
6 Idaho potatoes, scrubbed
Kosher salt
½ cup canola oil
Chopped fresh chives, for garnish (optional)
Fresh flat-leaf parsley leaves, for garnish (optional)

1. Combine the bay, celery salt, mustard, paprika, black and white peppers, nutmeg, cloves, allspice, ginger, chile flakes, and cardamom in a small bowl.

2. Put the potatoes in a pot of salted cold water, and bring to a boil. Reduce the heat and simmer until the potatoes are tender, but still firm, about 10 minutes. Drain and let cool before cutting each potato lengthwise into 8 thick slices or spears.

3. Heat your grill to high.

4. Brush the potatoes with the oil and season with the spice rub. Grill until golden brown on both sides and cooked through, 3 to 5 minutes. Serve sprinkled with chives and parsley, if desired.

Grilled New Potatoes and Zucchini with Radicchio, Goat Cheese, and Aged Sherry Vinaigrette

This colorful side dish hits all the right notes. The combination of tender new potatoes; mild zucchini; crisp, slightly bitter radicchio; and creamy, tangy goat cheese leaves nothing to be desired. Aged sherry vinegar has the depth of balsamic with just a little less sweetness. Sharp Dijon pulls together with the sherry and chopped shallot to make a bright, flavorful vinaigrette to bind all of the dish's elements together.

Serves 4 to 6

2½ pounds new red potatoes, scrubbed
Kosher salt
2 medium zucchini, scrubbed
1¼ cups olive oil
Freshly ground black pepper
½ cup aged sherry vinegar

2 teaspoons honey
1 small shallot, finely chopped
1 tablespoon Dijon mustard
2 medium heads of radicchio, coarsely chopped
6 ounces fresh goat cheese, crumbled
3 tablespoons finely chopped fresh chives

1. Put the potatoes in a pot of salted cold water and bring to a boil. Reduce the heat and simmer until the potatoes are tender, but still firm, about 8 minutes. Drain and let cool slightly.

2. Heat your grill to high.

3. Cut the potatoes and zucchini into ¼-inch-thick slices. Brush them on all sides with ½ cup of the oil and season with salt and pepper. Grill the potatoes and zucchini until golden brown and just cooked through, about 2 minutes per side for the potatoes and 3 minutes per side for the zucchini.

4. While the potatoes and zucchini are grilling, whisk together the vinegar, honey, shallot, and mustard in a medium bowl until combined. Slowly whisk in the remaining ¾ cup olive oil until emulsified. Season with salt and pepper.

5. Put the potatoes, zucchini, and radicchio in a bowl and gently toss with half of the vinaigrette. Season with salt and pepper. Transfer the potato mixture to a platter and top with the goat cheese. Drizzle with more of the dressing and sprinkle with the chopped chives.

Grilled Potatoes with Spicy Tomato Mayonnaise

Patatas bravas are found in just about every tapas bar in Spain and with good reason: they are addictively good. In the classic version, the potatoes are fried and served with a spicy tomato-garlic–based mayonnaise, but seeing as I have to find a way to get almost everything on the grill, I tried grilling the potatoes *and* the tomatoes for the aioli, and the results were fantastic. I also added my own touch in the form of smoky chipotle chiles, which are definitely not used in Spanish cuisine.

Serves 4

5 large red or yellow potatoes, scrubbed
Kosher salt
2 plum tomatoes
6 tablespoons olive oil
Freshly ground black pepper
1 cup mayonnaise

3 cloves garlic, chopped
2 teaspoons Spanish paprika
2 teaspoons pureed canned chipotle chiles
 in adobo
2 tablespoons finely chopped fresh flat-leaf
 parsley leaves

1. Put the potatoes in a pot of salted cold water and bring to a boil. Reduce the heat and simmer until the potatoes are tender, but still firm, 12 to 15 minutes. Drain and let cool before cutting each potato into ¾-inch-thick slices.

2. Heat your grill to high.

3. Brush the tomatoes with 2 tablespoons of the oil and season with salt and pepper. Place the tomatoes on the grill and grill until charred on all sides and soft, about 10 minutes. Remove from the grill and coarsely chop. Keep the grill on.

4. Combine the tomatoes, mayonnaise, garlic, paprika, and chipotle puree in a food processor and process until smooth. Season with salt and pepper.

5. Brush the potato slices on both sides with the remaining 4 tablespoons oil and season with salt and pepper. Place the potatoes on the grill, close the cover, and grill until lightly golden brown and just cooked through, about 2 minutes per side.

6. Carefully transfer the potatoes to a platter and garnish with the parsley. Serve the mayonnaise drizzled over the potatoes or on the side.

Grilled Potato and Goat Cheese Napoleon with Balsamic-Basil Vinaigrette

A napoleon (in the culinary world, at least) originally referred to a dessert consisting of alternating layers of puff pastry and custard or some other sweet filling. These days it's any dish of stacked ingredients, whether they be savory or sweet. It doesn't take much more time or effort to slice and layer the potato and goat cheese in this manner, but the end result is really elegant in appearance. I also love the way each bite is dynamic in texture. This side dish really covers all of the bases: it has eye-appeal, is fun to eat, and has amazing flavor from the charred potatoes, tangy goat cheese, and sweet, fresh dressing.

Serves 4

5 large red potatoes, scrubbed
Kosher salt
¼ cup balsamic vinegar
1 clove garlic
2 teaspoons Dijon mustard
¼ cup fresh basil leaves

¾ cup olive oil
Freshly ground black pepper
8 ounces fresh goat cheese
3 tablespoons chopped fresh chives (optional)

1. Put the potatoes in a pot of salted cold water and bring to a boil. Reduce the heat and simmer until the potatoes are tender, but still firm, 12 to 15 minutes. Drain and let cool before cutting each potato into ½-inch-thick slices.

2. While the potatoes are cooking, combine the vinegar, garlic, mustard, basil, and ½ cup of the oil in a blender and blend until smooth. Season with salt and pepper.

3. Heat your grill to medium.

4. Brush the potato slices on both sides with the remaining ¼ cup oil and season with salt and pepper. Place the potatoes on the grill, close the cover, and grill until lightly golden brown and just cooked through, about 2 minutes per side.

5. Carefully transfer the potatoes to a flat surface. Make stacks by layering the following: 1 slice potato, 1 tablespoon goat cheese, 1 slice potato, 1 tablespoon goat cheese, 1 slice potato. Place the stacks back on the grill, close the cover, and grill until the cheese begins to melt, about 1 minute.

6. Transfer the potatoes to a platter, drizzle some of the vinaigrette on and around the potatoes, and sprinkle with the chives.

Grilled New Potato Salad with Bacon and Buttermilk Dressing

I love smashed potatoes with buttermilk and bacon, so why not take those same ingredients and turn them into a salad? This is sure to replace the egg-and-pickle-relish version of your childhood.

Serves 4

2½ pounds small red new potatoes, scrubbed
Kosher salt
8 ounces bacon, diced
½ cup buttermilk
2 tablespoons mayonnaise
2 tablespoons sour cream
1 tablespoon Dijon mustard

1 teaspoon onion powder
1 teaspoon garlic powder
Freshly ground black pepper
¼ cup canola oil
3 green onions, white and green parts, thinly sliced

1. Put the potatoes in a pot of salted cold water and bring to a boil. Reduce the heat and simmer until the potatoes are tender but not cooked through, about 8 minutes. Drain the potatoes and let cool before cutting in half.

2. While the potatoes are cooking, cook the bacon in a large nonstick sauté pan over medium heat until golden brown and crisp, 8 to 10 minutes. Remove the bacon with a slotted spoon to a plate lined with paper towels.

3. Whisk together the buttermilk, mayonnaise, sour cream, and mustard in a large bowl and season with salt and pepper.

4. Heat your grill to medium.

5. Brush the potatoes on both sides with the oil and season with salt and pepper. Place the potatoes on the grill, cut side down, and grill until lightly golden brown, about 3 minutes. Turn the potatoes over and continue grilling until just cooked through, about 3 minutes longer.

6. Transfer the potatoes to the bowl with the dressing, add the bacon and green onions, and toss to coat. Serve warm or cover and refrigerate until cold, at least 2 hours or up to 8 hours.

Vinegar and Salt Grilled Potato "Chips"

I can eat an entire bag of salt and vinegar potato chips in a sitting. These "chips" may not have the crunch factor of the bagged variety, but they definitely have the taste factor going on. Be sure that the grill is heated only to medium when grilling the potato slices. You want them to cook slowly and get a really nice golden brown color on the outside; you don't want them charred.

Serves 4

4 large Yukon Gold potatoes, scrubbed
Kosher salt
¼ cup canola oil

Freshly ground black pepper
Malt vinegar

1. Heat your grill to medium.

2. Put the potatoes in a pot of salted cold water and bring to a boil. Reduce the heat and simmer until the potatoes are tender, but still firm, about 10 minutes. Drain and let cool before cutting into ¼-inch-thick slices.

3. Brush the potatoes on both sides with the oil and season with salt and pepper. Grill the slices until golden brown on both sides and just cooked through, about 10 minutes.

4. Remove the slices to a platter in an even layer and immediately drizzle with some vinegar and more salt.

Grilled Sweet Potato Wedges with Spicy Cranberry-Bourbon Glaze

I use sweet potatoes in everything—tamales, polenta, gratins—because I just love them. Even though the flavors in this recipe scream Thanksgiving, I eat these slightly sweet, slightly spicy, slightly tangy, ruby-glazed sweet potatoes all year long.

Serves 4

4 medium sweet potatoes, scrubbed
Kosher salt
3 cups cranberry juice or water
⅓ cup packed light brown sugar

½ teaspoon ground cinnamon
¼ teaspoon cayenne pepper
2 tablespoons bourbon
¼ cup canola oil

1. Put the potatoes in a pot of salted cold water and bring to a boil. Reduce the heat and simmer until the potatoes are tender, but still firm, about 15 minutes. Drain and let cool before quartering each potato lengthwise.

2. While the potatoes are cooking, combine the cranberry juice, brown sugar, cinnamon, cayenne, and ¼ teaspoon salt in a medium saucepan and bring to a boil over high heat. Cook, stirring occasionally, until the mixture is thickened and reduced to ¾ cup, about 10 minutes. Stir in the bourbon and let cook for 1 minute longer. Remove from the heat and let cool slightly.

3. Heat your grill to high.

4. Brush the potato wedges on both sides with the oil and season with salt. Grill, brushing with the cranberry glaze every 30 seconds, until lightly golden brown on both sides and just cooked through, about 6 minutes.

salmon

Perfectly Grilled Salmon • Grilled Salmon with Green Olive Relish • Grilled Salmon with Harissa • Grilled Salmon with Oregano Oil, Avocado Tzatziki Sauce, and Grilled Lemons • Grilled Salmon with Cherry Tomato, Charred Corn, and Basil Relish • San Diego–Style Blue Corn Salmon Tacos with Orange-Habanero Hot Sauce • Grilled Salmon with Honey-Mustard-Mint Sauce • Grilled Salmon with Miso-Orange Glaze • Grilled Salmon with Salsa Vera Cruz and Toasted Pumpkin Seeds

One of my favorite food memories from filming *Food Nation* for **Food Network** is of the incredible cedar-planked salmon that was prepared for me in the Pacific Northwest. The salmon tasted of the sea and the forest all at once, and it was impossible not to taste the wildness of the fish with each bite. When it's in season May through September, real wild Pacific salmon is a catch you have to seek out. It's more deeply flavored and cleaner than the farmed Atlantic varieties that fill the markets the rest of the year. That being said, farmed salmon is a reliably good, if second best, choice.

Salmon is one of the most popular fish in America, and I see that firsthand in my restaurants, where it is ordered more than any other fish. Rich and buttery, it's strong enough to team with deep, earthy flavors while pairing just as beautifully with bright, acidic components. Naturally high in heart-healthy Omega-3 oils, salmon is popular as much for its taste as for its health benefits.

The first key to great salmon is to make sure that you are getting only the freshest, firmest cuts available. As with any fish, salmon should never smell "fishy" but should rather smell slightly briny and like the sea itself. If you can see the whole fish, check out its eyes; they should be clear and bright, never cloudy.

With its firm flesh, salmon is a natural choice for the grill. It holds its shape well regardless of whether you are preparing steaks, fillets, or the whole fish. I also like to grill it because of the dynamic textures so easily achieved. I think salmon is best prepared medium-rare to medium. A forkful of grilled salmon with its slightly charred exterior giving way to a soft, buttery inside—it's simply a beautiful thing.

Perfectly Grilled Salmon

People are always asking me the secret to grilling salmon and other fish: Is it to oil the grill? Cook it on foil? Use a special basket? My answer: None of the above. It's pretty simple, really. Make sure that you start with a clean grill and then . . . leave the fish alone! If you try to flip your salmon before a crust has formed on the outside, the flesh will tear and fall apart. Let the fillets sit on the grill undisturbed for three to four minutes on the first side and you should be good to go, with easy flipping ahead. While this is a matter of personal preference to some degree, I think that salmon is best cooked no more than medium for optimal moistness. If you've tried it only well-done, try taking it off the grill just a little sooner than you usually do; I think you'll like the results.

Serves 4

4 (8-ounce) salmon fillets
2 tablespoons olive oil

Kosher salt and freshly ground black pepper

1. Heat your grill to high.

2. Brush the salmon fillets on both sides with the oil and season with salt and pepper. Place the fillets on the grill, skin side down, and grill until golden brown and slightly charred, 3 to 4 minutes. Flip the fillets over and continue grilling for 2 to 3 minutes for medium. The fish should feel slightly firm in the center and will register 140 degrees F on an instant-read thermometer.

Grilled Salmon with Green Olive Relish

With their crisp texture and fresh, nutty taste, picholine olives are too good to be just a cocktail offering. Provençal cooks use their native olives in preparations both raw and cooked with great success and I've taken my cue from them in making this zesty relish with lemon, garlic, parsley, thyme, and extra-virgin olive oil. Bright in flavor and in consistency, the relish is a wonderful counterpoint to rich and silky grilled salmon.

Serves 4

1 cup picholine olives, pitted and coarsely chopped
2 cloves garlic, finely chopped
2 teaspoons grated lemon zest
2 tablespoons extra-virgin olive oil
2 teaspoons finely chopped fresh thyme leaves

¼ cup coarsely chopped fresh flat-leaf parsley leaves
Kosher salt and freshly ground black pepper
Perfectly Grilled Salmon (page 189)

190

1. Combine the olives, garlic, zest, oil, thyme, and parsley in a small bowl and season with salt and pepper. Let sit at room temperature for at least 30 minutes before serving or cover and refrigerate for up to 2 days. If making in advance, do not add the thyme and parsley until just before serving. Serve chilled or at room temperature.

2. Transfer the fish to plates and top with some of the relish.

Grilled Salmon with Harissa

Harissa, also known as Tunisian hot sauce, is a fiery, rust-colored condiment made from bell peppers, chiles, and garlic that is traditionally stirred into the broth ladled over couscous. It is also great as a marinade for beef or chicken. Commercially prepared harissa is available at specialty stores in the United States, but homemade harissa is easy to prepare, has a fresher taste, and allows you to control the heat. Serve this salmon over steamed rice for a healthy and flavorful dinner or lunch.

Serves 4

4 tablespoons canola oil

3 cloves garlic, chopped

3 chile de árbol chiles, stems removed, or 1 teaspoon red chile flakes

2 red bell peppers, grilled (see page 120), peeled, seeded, and chopped

1 plum tomato, grilled (see page 120), seeded, and chopped

1 teaspoon caraway seeds, toasted (see page 19)

1 teaspoon coriander seeds, toasted (see page 19)

Kosher salt and freshly ground black pepper

2 tablespoons aged sherry vinegar

2 teaspoons honey

4 (8-ounce) salmon fillets

2 tablespoons finely chopped fresh cilantro leaves

1. Heat 2 tablespoons of the oil in a saucepan over medium heat. Add the garlic and chiles and cook until the garlic is soft and the chiles are slightly toasted, about 1 minute. Add the bell peppers, tomato, caraway, and coriander; season with salt and pepper; and cook until the mixture is heated through and the tomato becomes very soft and starts to break down, 8 to 10 minutes.

2. Transfer the mixture to a food processor, add the vinegar and honey, and process until smooth. Transfer to a bowl and let cool to room temperature. The harissa can be made 2 days in advance, covered, and refrigerated. Bring to room temperature before using.

3. Heat your grill to high.

4. Brush the salmon on both sides with the remaining 2 tablespoons oil and season with salt. Brush the skin side of the salmon with some of the harissa and place on the grill, harissa side down. Grill until light golden brown and a crust has formed, 3 to 4 minutes. Turn the fish over and brush the top of the salmon with more of the harissa and continue grilling until just cooked through, 2 to 3 minutes.

5. Remove the salmon to a platter and sprinkle with the chopped cilantro.

Grilled Salmon with Oregano Oil, Avocado Tzatziki Sauce, and Grilled Lemons

Salmon, not being native to the Mediterranean, is not typically used in Greek cuisine, but I like the flavor pairing here; the rich salmon stands up nicely to the pungent tzatziki. I also like brushing the salmon with the oregano-spiked oil instead of marinating the fish because the herb-infused oil kind of acts as an instant marinade. While I always love traditional tzatziki, the additions of avocado and serrano chile work quite well. Rich and creamy avocado rounds out the sauce, providing a natural balance to the tangy yogurt and sharp garlic. As for the serrano, well, a touch of heat never hurt anything in my book! See photograph on page 186.

Serves 4

¼ cup plus 2 tablespoons olive oil
2 tablespoons fresh oregano leaves
Kosher salt and freshly ground black pepper

4 (6-ounce) salmon fillets
2 lemons, halved
Avocado Tzatziki (recipe follows)

1. Heat your grill to high.

2. Combine ¼ cup of the oil and the oregano in a blender and blend until smooth. Season with salt and pepper.

3. Brush the fillets on both sides with some of the oregano oil and season with salt and pepper. Grill the salmon for about 3 minutes per side, until slightly charred and cooked to medium, brushing with more of the oil every 30 seconds.

4. While the fish is grilling, brush the cut sides of the lemons with the remaining 2 tablespoons olive oil and grill, cut side down, until lightly golden brown, 2 minutes.

5. Serve the fillets with a dollop of avocado tzatziki and squeeze the juice from the grilled lemons on top.

Avocado Tzatziki

Makes 1 cup

2 ripe Hass avocados, peeled, pitted, and
 chopped
2 cloves garlic, chopped
1 serrano chile, chopped
¼ cup Greek yogurt

Grated zest and juice of 1 small lemon
½ English cucumber, finely diced
¼ cup chopped fresh flat-leaf parsley leaves
Kosher salt and freshly ground black pepper

Put the avocados, garlic, serrano, yogurt, lemon zest, and lemon juice in the bowl of
a food processor and process until smooth. Transfer the mixture to a medium bowl,
stir in the cucumber and parsley, and season with salt and pepper. Cover and refrigerate for at least 30 minutes and up to 2 hours before serving.

Grilled Salmon with Cherry Tomato, Charred Corn, and Basil Relish

This dish is so simple that you can prepare it in less than fifteen minutes and so flavorful and impressive looking on the plate that you could serve it for a dinner party and look like a star. I just love the combination of tomatoes, corn, and basil and feel they pair particularly well with fish, especially salmon. You can substitute almost any other herb for the basil; tarragon, parsley, and even my favorite, cilantro, would all work well.

Serves 4

4 ears Perfectly Grilled Corn (page 83)
2 tablespoons canola oil
Kosher salt and freshly ground black pepper
1 pint cherry or grape tomatoes, halved
3 tablespoons extra-virgin olive oil

2 tablespoons balsamic vinegar
3 tablespoons thinly sliced basil leaves, plus
   whole basil sprigs, for garnish
Perfectly Grilled Salmon (page 189)

1. Heat your grill to high.

2. Brush the corn with the canola oil on all sides and season with salt and pepper. Grill until charred on all sides, about 8 minutes. Remove the cobs from the grill and let cool slightly. Remove the kernels from the cobs (see page 83) and transfer to a medium bowl. Add the tomatoes, olive oil, vinegar, and sliced basil and season with salt and pepper. Let the relish sit at room temperature for 15 minutes before serving.

3. Spoon the relish onto 4 plates and top with the salmon fillets. Garnish with basil sprigs.

San Diego–Style Blue Corn Salmon Tacos with Orange-Habanero Hot Sauce

Fish tacos are a staple of California Mexican food, and San Diego especially has some amazing offerings. To the uninitiated, a fish taco might sound a little strange, but really they are mild, fresh, and delicious. I like to prepare a sort of salmon salad, combining grilled and flaked salmon with crunchy cabbage, green onions, and a smoky chipotle mayonnaise, to tuck into blue corn taco shells. The orange-habanero hot sauce is one of my favorites—spicy, but flavorful. The orange juice echoes the spicy, fruity taste of the habanero.

Serves 4 to 6

3 (8-ounce) salmon fillets, cooked as for
  Perfectly Grilled Salmon (page 189)
¼ head of green cabbage, finely shredded
3 green onions, green and white parts, thinly sliced
1 cup mayonnaise
1 tablespoon pureed canned chipotle chiles in
  adobo

Grated zest of 1 lime
1 tablespoon fresh lime juice
Kosher salt
¼ cup finely chopped fresh cilantro leaves
12 fried blue corn taco shells
Orange-Habanero Hot Sauce (recipe follows)

1. Remove the salmon from the grill and let cool slightly. Shred the meat with a fork and place in a bowl with the cabbage and green onions.

2. Whisk together the mayonnaise, chipotle puree, lime zest, and lime juice in a small bowl and season with salt. Add the mayonnaise mixture and the cilantro to the salmon mixture and gently fold to combine. Season the mixture with salt to taste, if needed.

3. Divide the salmon mixture among the taco shells and drizzle each with the orange-habanero sauce.

Orange-Habanero Hot Sauce

Makes approximately 1 cup

1 quart orange juice (not from concentrate)
1 habanero chile

2 tablespoons honey
Kosher salt

1. Pour the juice into a medium nonreactive saucepan. Make a few slits in the habanero with a paring knife and add to the juice. Bring the juice to a boil over high heat and cook, stirring occasionally, until reduced to 1 cup, 20 to 25 minutes.

2. Remove the habanero and discard. Whisk in the honey and season with salt. Let cool to room temperature before serving. The sauce can be made 2 days in advance, covered, and refrigerated. Bring to room temperature before serving.

Grilled Salmon with Honey-Mustard-Mint Sauce

On just about every single brunch buffet you will find whole salmon (normally poached) on a bed of watercress with a small bowl of mustard sauce next to it for spooning over the fish. And while I help myself to a portion, as I eat it I always think about how much better the dish would be if the salmon were grilled with a golden brown crust and the mustard sauce had a bit more flavor. So here's my version . . . maybe you will serve it at your next brunch.

Serves 4

¼ cup Dijon mustard
2 tablespoons whole-grain mustard
3 tablespoons honey
2 tablespoons prepared horseradish, drained
2 tablespoons finely chopped fresh mint leaves
Kosher salt and freshly ground black pepper

1 bunch of watercress, coarsely chopped
1 small red onion, halved and thinly sliced
2 tablespoons aged sherry vinegar
2 tablespoons extra-virgin olive oil
Perfectly Grilled Salmon (page 189)

1. Whisk together both of the mustards, the honey, horseradish, mint, ¼ teaspoon salt, and ¼ teaspoon pepper in a small bowl. Let sit for at least 15 minutes before using. The sauce can be made 1 day in advance and refrigerated but do not add the mint until just before using. Bring to room temperature before serving.

2. Combine the watercress and onion in a medium bowl, add the vinegar and oil, and season with salt and pepper. Toss to combine. Transfer the salad to a platter, top with the salmon fillets, and drizzle each fillet with the mustard sauce.

Grilled Salmon with Miso-Orange Glaze

While not at all complicated, this glaze manages to pull off a whole lot in terms of flavor. Miso (fermented soybean paste) is nutty and rich and adds a complex taste to the glaze while orange juice and zest keep it fresh and bright. The naturally sweet orange juice needs only a couple of tablespoons of brown sugar to make the glaze deep and luscious. Soy sauce and rice wine vinegar echo the Asian flavor of the miso. Miso is most often found in the dairy aisle of your supermarket or can be purchased online.

Serves 4

2 cups orange juice (not from concentrate)
Grated zest of 1 orange
2 tablespoons light brown sugar
⅓ cup yellow miso paste
1 tablespoon low-sodium soy sauce

1 tablespoon rice wine vinegar
4 (8-ounce) salmon fillets
Kosher salt and freshly ground black pepper
2 green onions, white and green parts, thinly sliced

1. Combine the orange juice and zest and brown sugar in a medium saucepan and bring to a boil over high heat. Simmer, stirring occasionally, until thickened and reduced to ½ cup, about 10 minutes. Whisk in the miso and cook for 1 minute. Remove from the heat, whisk in the soy sauce and vinegar, and let cool to room temperature.

2. Place the salmon in a baking dish, pour half of the glaze over the fillets, and turn to coat. Let marinate at room temperature for 15 minutes.

3. Heat your grill to high.

4. Remove the salmon from the marinade and season with salt and pepper. Place on the grill and grill until golden brown and slightly charred, 3 to 4 minutes. Turn the fillets over, brush with the remaining glaze, and grill until cooked to medium, 2 to 3 minutes longer.

5. Transfer the salmon to a plate and garnish with the green onions.

Grilled Salmon with Salsa Vera Cruz and Toasted Pumpkin Seeds

Salsa Vera Cruz is a traditional Mexican sauce for seafood. It's an incredibly fresh, slightly spicy tomato-based sauce loaded with flavor in the form of olives, capers, garlic, and jalapeños. While Salsa Vera Cruz is usually served with red snapper, I think salmon works very well as the fresh, slightly briny flavors of the sauce really cut through the rich nature of the fish. Toasted pumpkin seeds add a nice, earthy crunch.

Serves 4

6 plum tomatoes
2 tablespoons canola oil
Kosher salt and freshly ground black pepper
1 small red onion, halved and thinly sliced
2 cloves garlic, finely chopped
½ cup green olives, pitted and halved
2 pickled jalapeño chiles, drained and thinly sliced

2 tablespoons capers, drained
1 tablespoon finely chopped fresh oregano leaves
2 teaspoons finely chopped fresh thyme leaves
¼ cup extra-virgin olive oil
¼ cup pumpkin seeds, toasted (see page 19)
Perfectly Grilled Salmon (page 189)
Fresh thyme sprigs, for garnish

1. Heat your grill to high.

2. Put the tomatoes in a bowl with the canola oil, season with salt and pepper, and toss to coat. Place on the grill and cook until charred on all sides and soft, 8 to 10 minutes.

3. Remove the tomatoes from the grill and coarsely chop them. Transfer to a bowl, immediately add the onion, garlic, olives, jalapeños, capers, oregano, thyme, and olive oil, and stir to combine. Season with salt and pepper. Let the salsa sit at room temperature for at least 15 minutes and up to 1 hour before serving. Stir in the pumpkin seeds just before serving.

4. Place the salmon on plates and spoon the salsa over the fish. Garnish with thyme sprigs.

scallops

Perfectly Grilled Sea Scallops • Grilled Sea Scallops on Tortilla Chips with Avocado Puree and Jalapeño Pesto • Grilled Sea Scallops with Green Onion Relish and Warm Bacon Vinaigrette • Grilled Sea Scallops with Fresh Corn–Basil Sauce and Grilled Tomato Relish • Grilled Sea Scallops with Grilled Tomato Vinaigrette • Grilled Scallops with Citrus-Ginger Sauce and Rice Noodle Salad • Coriander-Spiced Sea Scallops with Green Pea–Cilantro Sauce

I love to serve scallops at the restaurants and at home. Sweet, mild, plump, and tender, fresh scallops are such crowd pleasers, even for people who might think that they don't like seafood. They're also quite easy to prepare, especially on the grill. Just be sure to keep their cooking time brief to ensure that they stay juicy, not tough.

There are a few kinds of scallops out there, but what you will see in your market will be labeled as either bay or sea scallops. While I love bay (or Nantucket) scallops, their diminutive size makes them unsuitable for the grill. The larger sea scallops are usually about an inch to an inch and a half across, though you certainly may come across much bigger ones. You may also see scallops labeled "diver scallops" both in your market and on restaurant menus. This refers to the way in which the scallops were harvested. They are hand picked by divers, as opposed to the conventional collecting method of chain dredging. Scallops collected this way will be less gritty, because the sea floor isn't disturbed as it is with the chain sweeping, and they have the additional benefit of being ecologically friendly. But keep in mind that this is a labor-intensive process with a fairly small yield and as a result, diver scallops are very expensive.

Almost all scallops are shucked on the boat and you will very rarely see them in the shell. They are easy to shuck yourself if you find them, but I don't think that it's necessary. Do beware of shucked scallops that are overly shiny and white. These "wet" scallops have probably been treated with an additive to act as a preservative and to help the scallops retain water so they will weigh more for sale. Untreated or "dry" scallops will be cream-colored to slightly pinkish or beige and will have a slight, appealing sheen, not a shiny gloss. As with any seafood, don't be afraid to ask to smell what you are buying. They should smell slightly sweet and mildly of the sea. Also remember to remove the small, tough muscle found on one side of each scallop before grilling. If you don't peel off this piece from the scallop, you'll have an extremely tough and chewy piece attached to your tender scallop after cooking.

Perfectly Grilled Sea Scallops

I love the fresh briny and sweet taste of scallops, especially when they are grilled. The direct heat of the grill caramelizes the outside of the scallop, making it even sweeter. Even though scallops have a very meaty texture, they can be extremely fragile on the grill, so be sure to oil them well before putting them on the grates of the grill and make sure the grill is extremely hot. This will help ensure that the scallops won't stick or tear.

Serves 4

1 pound sea scallops (about 20), muscle
    removed

¼ cup olive or canola oil
Kosher salt and freshly ground black pepper

1. Heat your grill to high.

2. Brush the scallops on both sides with the oil, making sure that they are well coated, and season with salt and pepper. Place the scallops on the grill and grill until golden brown and slightly charred, about 3 minutes. Turn over and continue cooking for 2 to 3 minutes longer until just cooked through.

Grilled Sea Scallops on Tortilla Chips with Avocado Puree and Jalapeño Pesto

This is such a great recipe to serve at your next outdoor cocktail party. It goes perfectly with margaritas, beer, or a crisp white wine and is so easy to prepare that you can make it in less than thirty minutes. If scallops aren't available or aren't your thing, shrimp is a perfect substitute.

Serves 4

2 ripe Hass avocados, peeled, pitted, and coarsely chopped
3 tablespoons chopped red onion
Juice of 2 limes
2 tablespoons canola oil
¼ cup chopped fresh cilantro leaves, plus extra whole leaves for serving

Kosher salt and freshly ground black pepper
10 blue corn tortilla chips
10 yellow corn tortilla chips
Perfectly Grilled Sea Scallops (page 205)
Jalapeño Pesto (recipe follows)

1. Combine the avocados, onion, lime juice, oil, chopped cilantro, and salt and pepper to taste in a food processor and process until smooth. Scrape into a bowl.

2. Spread about a tablespoon of avocado puree over each chip. Top the puree with a scallop and top each scallop with some of the jalapeño pesto. Garnish with cilantro leaves.

Jalapeño Pesto

Makes about ¾ cup

1½ cups packed fresh cilantro leaves
6 jalapeño chiles, grilled (see page 120), peeled, and chopped
1 clove garlic, chopped

2 tablespoons pine nuts
Kosher salt and freshly ground black pepper
½ cup extra-virgin olive oil

Combine the cilantro, jalapeños, garlic, pine nuts, and salt and pepper to taste in a food processor and process until coarsely chopped. With the motor running, slowly add the oil and process until smooth and emulsified. Scrape into a bowl. The pesto can be made 2 days in advance, covered, and refrigerated. Bring to room temperature before serving.

Grilled Sea Scallops with Green Onion Relish and Warm Bacon Vinaigrette

I never really understood that classic dish of scallops wrapped in bacon; it seems to me that neither can be cooked properly together. Because scallops take only a few minutes to cook, it always seems that the bacon, which takes longer to cook, is normally underdone. This recipe is my solution. Crispy bacon relish tops perfectly grilled scallops and that wonderful bacon fat left behind after the bacon is cooked makes a slightly salty, slightly sweet dressing.

Serves 4

3 tablespoons olive oil
8 ounces bacon, cut into small dice
2 green onions, white and green parts, halved lengthwise and thinly sliced
2 shallots, finely diced
¼ cup apple cider vinegar or white wine vinegar

2 teaspoons sugar
2 teaspoons Dijon mustard
2 teaspoons finely chopped fresh thyme leaves
Kosher salt and freshly ground black pepper
Perfectly Grilled Sea Scallops (page 205)

1. Heat 1 tablespoon of the oil in a medium sauté pan over medium heat. Add the bacon and cook until golden brown and crisp, 8 to 10 minutes. Remove the bacon with a slotted spoon to a plate lined with paper towels to drain. Transfer the bacon to a small bowl, stir in the green onions, and set aside. (Reserve the bacon fat in the pan.)

2. Increase the heat under the pan to high, add the shallots, and cook until soft, about 2 minutes. Add the vinegar and sugar, bring to a boil, and cook until the sugar is dissolved. Remove from the heat, stir in the mustard and thyme, and season with salt and pepper.

3. Transfer the scallops to a platter, drizzle with the warm bacon vinaigrette, and top each scallop with some of the green onion relish.

Grilled Sea Scallops with Fresh Corn–Basil Sauce and Grilled Tomato Relish

This dish is a celebration of summer if I've ever seen one. The combination of basil, corn, and tomatoes is just so good atop sea scallops—it's all of summer's best elements in one dish bursting with color, flavor, and texture. For the rich, creamy base, sweet pureed corn has so much natural creaminess that a mere quarter cup of cream is all you need to make the sauce totally decadent. Top that with succulent scallops and fresh relish to make each bite a delightful study in contrasts, yet total taste harmony.

Serves 4

Grilled Tomato Relish
6 ripe plum tomatoes
5 tablespoons olive oil
Kosher salt and freshly ground black pepper
1 small red onion, finely diced
2 cloves garlic, finely chopped
2 tablespoons balsamic vinegar
¼ cup finely chopped fresh basil leaves

Fresh Corn–Basil Sauce
2 tablespoons olive oil
1 Spanish onion, coarsely chopped
8 ears fresh corn, shucked and kernels removed from the cobs (see page 83)
2 (14.5-ounce) cans low-sodium chicken or vegetable broth
2 teaspoons sugar
Kosher salt and freshly ground black pepper
¼ cup heavy cream
12 fresh basil leaves, cut into thin ribbons

Perfectly Grilled Sea Scallops (page 205)
Fresh basil sprigs, for garnish

1. Heat your grill to high.

2. To make the relish, place the tomatoes in a bowl, toss with 2 tablespoons of the oil, and season with salt and pepper. Place the tomatoes on the grill and grill until charred on all sides and just cooked through, about 10 minutes.

3. Remove the tomatoes from the grill and coarsely chop. Put the chopped tomatoes in a bowl; add the remaining 3 tablespoons oil, the onion, garlic, vinegar, and chopped basil; and gently mix until combined. Let sit at room temperature for 30 minutes or cover and refrigerate for up to 4 hours. Bring to room temperature before serving.

4. To make the sauce, heat the oil in a large saucepan over high heat. Add the onion and cook until soft, 4 to 5 minutes. Add the corn and cook for 1 minute. Add the broth and sugar, season with salt and pepper, and bring to a boil. Cook until the corn is very tender, about 30 minutes.

5. Transfer the corn mixture to a blender with a slotted spoon, add half of the cooking liquid, and blend until smooth. Reserve the extra liquid. Strain the sauce through a medium mesh strainer, pressing on the solids, into a clean saucepan and bring to a simmer over medium heat. If the mixture is too thick, thin with some of the remaining liquid. Stir in the heavy cream and cook until the sauce thickens slightly, 4 to 5 minutes. Remove from the heat and stir in the basil.

6. Ladle the sauce onto 4 dinner plates. Divide the scallops around the perimeter of the plates and place some of the relish in the center. Garnish with basil sprigs.

Grilled Sea Scallops with Grilled Tomato Vinaigrette

This dish is based on the classic scallop dish from Provence, France, called scallops Provençale. The cuisine of Provence is very distinct from the rest of French cooking. A Mediterranean influence results in an abundance of fresh seafood and fresh produce, and many dishes make use of tomatoes, garlic, fresh herbs, and lots of olive oil.

Serves 4

6 plum tomatoes
6 tablespoons extra-virgin olive oil
Kosher salt and freshly ground black pepper
2 cloves garlic, finely chopped
¼ cup Niçoise olives, pitted and chopped

1 tablespoon finely chopped fresh thyme leaves
4 tablespoons coarsely chopped fresh basil leaves
Perfectly Grilled Sea Scallops (page 205)

1. Heat your grill to high.

2. Brush the tomatoes with 2 tablespoons of the oil and season with salt and pepper. Place the tomatoes on the grill and grill on all sides until slightly charred and soft, 8 to 10 minutes. Remove the tomatoes from the grill, let cool slightly, and then cut into small dice.

3. Put the tomatoes in a medium bowl and immediately add the garlic, olives, thyme, 3 tablespoons of the basil, and the remaining 4 tablespoons olive oil. Season with salt and pepper. Let sit at room temperature for at least 15 minutes and up to 1 hour before serving. Do not refrigerate.

4. Spoon half of the vinaigrette onto a platter and top with the scallops. Spoon the remaining vinaigrette over the top of the scallops and sprinkle with the remaining tablespoon of basil.

Grilled Scallops with Citrus-Ginger Sauce and Rice Noodle Salad

Rice noodles, soft and translucent, are light in taste and texture and are a nice change of pace when you're tired of regular pasta or plain rice. Used all over Asia, they are also a natural paired with the Asian-inspired citrus-ginger sauce in this recipe. See photograph on page 202.

Serves 4

2 teaspoons toasted sesame oil
4 tablespoons canola oil
2 tablespoons grated orange zest
12 large sea scallops, muscle removed
1 tablespoon finely grated peeled fresh ginger
½ teaspoon red chile flakes
2 cups orange juice (not from concentrate)
Juice of 1 lime
2 tablespoons light brown sugar

1 tablespoon low-sodium soy sauce
2 tablespoons rice wine vinegar
Kosher salt
8 ounces rice noodles
Freshly ground black pepper
2 green onions, white and green parts, thinly sliced
1 tablespoon sesame seeds, toasted (see page 19)

1. Whisk together the sesame oil, 2 tablespoons of the canola oil, and the orange zest in a medium bowl. Add the scallops and let marinate in the refrigerator for at least 15 minutes and up to 30 minutes.

2. Heat the remaining 2 tablespoons canola oil in a medium saucepan over medium heat. Add the ginger and red chile flakes and cook until the ginger is soft, about 2 minutes. Increase the heat to high, add the orange juice, lime juice, brown sugar, and soy sauce, and simmer, stirring occasionally, until the mixture is reduced by half, 8 to 10 minutes. Remove from the heat, stir in the rice vinegar, and let cool to room temperature. The sauce can be made 8 hours in advance, covered, and refrigerated. Bring to room temperature before serving.

3. Bring a large pot of salted water to a boil over high heat. Add the noodles and cook until al dente, 3 to 4 minutes. Drain, rinse with cold water, and drain again. Transfer to a platter and toss with half of the citrus-ginger sauce.

4. Heat your grill to high.

5. Season the scallops on both sides with salt and pepper. Place the scallops on the grill and grill until golden brown and slightly charred, about 3 minutes. Turn over and continue cooking for about 3 minutes longer until just cooked through.

6. Place the scallops on top of the noodles and drizzle with the remaining citrus-ginger sauce. Garnish with green onions and sesame seeds.

Coriander-Spiced Sea Scallops with Green Pea–Cilantro Sauce

Cilantro is often mistakenly referred to as coriander but they are two different things. Coriander is the seed (which is used as a spice) from which cilantro (the herb) is grown. While the flavors are completely different, when used together, they complement each other beautifully.

Serves 4

2 cups frozen peas, thawed
3 tablespoons red wine vinegar
¼ cup lightly packed fresh cilantro leaves, plus more for garnish
⅓ to ½ cup extra-virgin olive oil
Kosher salt and freshly ground black pepper

Honey, to taste
1 tablespoon ground coriander
1 pound sea scallops (about 20), muscle removed
¼ cup canola oil

1. Combine the peas, vinegar, cilantro, and a few tablespoons water in a blender and blend until smooth. With the motor running, slowly add the extra-virgin olive oil and puree until emulsified. Season with salt, pepper, and honey. If the mixture is too thick to pour, thin with a little water.

2. Heat your grill to high.

3. Stir together the coriander, 2 teaspoons salt, and 1 teaspoon pepper in a small bowl. Brush the scallops on both sides with the canola oil, making sure that they are well coated, and season with the coriander mixture. Place the scallops on the grill and grill until golden brown and slightly charred, about 3 minutes. Turn over and continue cooking 2 to 3 minutes longer until just cooked through.

4. Spoon some of the sauce onto a medium platter, top with the scallops, and garnish with cilantro leaves.

shrimp

Perfectly Grilled Shrimp • Grilled Shrimp with Gazpacho Bread Salad • All-You-Can-Eat Shrimp with Green Onion, Garlic, and BBQ Spices • Grilled Shrimp with Smoked Chile "Cocktail" Sauce • Grilled Shrimp with Lemon-Basil Dipping Sauce • Sherry Vinegar–Marinated Shrimp Wrapped in Serrano Ham with Piquillo Dipping Sauce • Pickled Grilled Shrimp • Grilled Spice-Rubbed Shrimp "Niçoise" Salad • Grilled Shrimp with Tomatillo-Horseradish Sauce

Sweet, plump, and petite, shrimp are favorite party fare. Have you ever seen a crowd attack a platter of shrimp cocktail? Too often, though, those shrimp are poached beyond tenderness, making them tough and flavorless. Grilling shrimp brings out their best: the grill's shot of heat intensifies their natural sweet quality. Just keep the cooking time brief so they're juicy, and you've got it made.

There are many different kinds of shrimp on the market: freshwater, warm-water, cold-water, and saltwater varieties. Most shrimp is sold frozen, but you will occasionally be able to find fresh shrimp in markets local to their origins, from Maine to Florida. When you can, I say try it; fresh shrimp are delicious. That being said, I think that frozen shrimp can be very good, too. I prefer to purchase wild American shrimp whenever possible (fresh or frozen), but that does not make up the majority of what's on the market. Much of what you'll find is from overseas and/or farmed. Talk to your fishmonger, read your labels, and do what you can to avoid shrimp that have been loaded with preservatives or treated with antibiotics. It's a health matter, sure, but it's also about taste. Treated shrimp often have a chemical aftertaste. Also do what you can to make sure that frozen shrimp haven't been defrosted for too long when you're purchasing them, as shrimp are extremely perishable. It's a safe bet to buy them frozen and defrost them as you need them. You can keep well-wrapped frozen shrimp in your freezer for up to a couple of months.

I grill shrimp both in their shells and peeled, depending upon their size and how I plan on using them in their final presentation. Same thing goes for their heads. Provided you haven't bought them already peeled, don't throw away those shells and heads. Toss them in a plastic bag and freeze them; the next time you have a craving for shrimp bisque, the base for a delectable shrimp stock will be there waiting.

Shrimp Sizes

Extra colossal • fewer than 10 per pound

Colossal • fewer than 15 per pound

Extra jumbo • 16 to 20 per pound

Jumbo • 21 to 25 per pound

Extra large • 26 to 30 per pound

Large • 31 to 40 per pound

Medium-large • 36 to 40 per pound

Small • 1 to 60 per pound

Extra small • 61 to 70 per pound

Tiny • more than 70 per pound

Perfectly Grilled Shrimp

Grilling shrimp might just be one of the easiest things in the world. Seriously, toss them with a little oil, salt, and pepper; lay them out on the grill; turn; and they're done. Now, the key to doing it all well is to keep it short and sweet just like that. The total grilling time shouldn't exceed 3 to 4 minutes, and that can go by awfully quickly! You want to grill them until the flesh just turns pink—then it's off to the platter. Don't overcook them or you'll end up with something bland and rubbery as opposed to sweet and tender.

Serves 4

1 pound extra-large (26 to 30 count) shrimp, peeled and deveined
2 tablespoons canola oil

1 tablespoon kosher salt
2 teaspoons freshly ground black pepper

1. Heat your grill to high.

2. Put the shrimp in a large bowl. Toss the shrimp with the oil and season with the salt and pepper. Place the shrimp on the grates of the grill in an even layer and grill until golden brown and slightly charred, 1½ to 2 minutes. Turn the shrimp over and continue grilling until just cooked through, 45 seconds to 1 minute longer. Remove the shrimp to a platter.

Grilled Shrimp with Gazpacho Bread Salad

The addition of grilled shrimp turns any salad into a meal, especially one as flavorful and satisfying as this. The Italians may be famous for turning stale bread into a delicious salad with panzanella, but the Spanish are just as resourceful with their leftover bread, using it as the base for the original white gazpacho. I've married the two concepts here by making a gazpacho bread salad; it's the best of both worlds.

Serves 4

¼ cup aged sherry vinegar
1 small clove garlic, finely chopped
2 teaspoons Dijon mustard
2 teaspoons honey
Kosher salt and freshly ground black pepper
¾ cup extra-virgin olive oil
8 plum tomatoes
4 green onions, root ends trimmed
6 (1-inch-thick) slices day-old country-style white bread

¼ cup canola oil
1 large jarred roasted red bell pepper, seeded and diced
1 large jarred roasted yellow bell pepper, seeded and diced
½ red onion, thinly sliced
1 English cucumber, halved and diced
4 tablespoons chopped fresh flat-leaf parsley leaves
Perfectly Grilled Shrimp (page 219)

1. Whisk together the vinegar, garlic, mustard, honey, and salt and pepper to taste in a medium bowl until combined. Slowly whisk in the olive oil until emulsified. Let sit at room temperature while you prepare the salad. The vinaigrette can be made up to 8 hours in advance and refrigerated.

2. Heat your grill to high.

3. Brush the tomatoes, green onions, and bread on all sides with the canola oil and season with salt and pepper. Grill the tomatoes until slightly charred on all sides, 6 to 8 minutes. Grill the green onions until slightly charred and cooked through, 2 to 3 minutes per side. Grill the bread until lightly golden brown and crisp, 1 to 2 minutes per side.

4. Cut the tomatoes into quarters. Cut the green onions into thirds. Cut the bread into medium dice. Combine the tomatoes, green onions, red and yellow peppers, red onion, cucumber, and 2 tablespoons of the parsley in a large bowl, add half of the vinaigrette, and toss to coat. Let the mixture sit at room temperature for 15 minutes and then stir in the bread.

5. Transfer the bread salad to a large platter and top with the grilled shrimp. Drizzle with the remaining vinaigrette and garnish with the remaining 2 tablespoons parsley.

All-You-Can-Eat Shrimp with Green Onion, Garlic, and BBQ Spices

Nothing is more festive than a big platter of all-you-can-eat shrimp and a beer on a hot summer day. The spices used in the recipe are the same spices that you would normally find in a classic barbecue sauce. Of course, you can peel the shrimp before cooking them, but it won't be as much fun.

Serves 4 to 6

¼ cup smoked sweet paprika
2 tablespoons ancho chile powder
2 tablespoons light brown sugar
2 teaspoons ground cumin
2 teaspoons kosher salt
1 teaspoon freshly ground black pepper

2 pounds extra-large (26 to 30 count) shrimp, shell on
7 tablespoons canola oil
12 cloves garlic, coarsely chopped
½ cup thinly sliced green onion, white and green parts

1. Whisk together the paprika, ancho powder, brown sugar, cumin, salt, and pepper in a small bowl.

2. Put the shrimp in a large bowl, add the spice rub, and stir well to coat each shrimp.

3. Heat your grill to high.

4. Heat 3 tablespoons of the oil in a large cast-iron or stainless steel sauté pan on the grates of the grill. Add one-third of the shrimp and half of the garlic and cook until just cooked through, 3 to 4 minutes. Stir in one-third of the green onions and transfer to a large platter or turn out onto brown paper bags. Wipe out the pan with paper towels, and repeat with the remaining ingredients.

Grilled Shrimp with
Smoked Chile "Cocktail" Sauce

No matter how bland or rubbery the shrimp, or how uninspired the sauce, shrimp cocktail seems to remain everyone's favorite. Why not make it the star of the party, and not just the old standby? Replace plain boiled shrimp with gorgeously charred shrimp, hot off the grill, and turn that cocktail sauce on its head like I've done here. This sauce gets its kick from fresh and aromatic ingredients, such as peppery radishes, smoky chipotles, and refreshing lime juice. It beats anything from a bottle.

Serves 4

1¼ cups ketchup
2 tablespoons fresh lime juice
6 pink radishes, finely diced
1 large shallot, finely chopped
1 tablespoon pureed canned chipotle chiles in adobo

2 tablespoons prepared horseradish, drained
1 teaspoon honey
3 tablespoons finely chopped fresh cilantro leaves
Kosher salt and freshly ground black pepper
Perfectly Grilled Shrimp (page 219)

1. Whisk together the ketchup, lime juice, radishes, shallot, chipotle puree, horse-radish, honey, and cilantro in a medium bowl and season lightly with salt and pepper. Cover and refrigerate for at least 30 minutes before serving. The sauce can be made 8 hours in advance and refrigerated, but in that case do not add the cilantro until ready to serve.

2. To serve the shrimp, divide the sauce among 4 martini glasses and hang the shrimp from the rims.

Grilled Shrimp with Lemon-Basil Dipping Sauce

I can't think of two ingredients more suited to each other than lemon and basil. Both are so fresh and just taste like sunshine and summer—no matter what time of year it is. I make this dish to serve four people as an entrée, but it also works wonderfully as an hors d'oeuvre. Simply spear each shrimp with a toothpick and serve along-side a dish of the dipping sauce for easy elegance.

Serves 4

1 cup mayonnaise
¼ cup fresh basil leaves, chopped
Grated zest and juice of 1 lemon
2 anchovy fillets

½ teaspoon kosher salt
¼ teaspoon freshly ground black pepper
Perfectly Grilled Shrimp (page 219)

1. Combine the mayonnaise, basil, lemon zest and juice, anchovies, salt, and pepper in a food processor and process until smooth. Cover and refrigerate for at least 1 hour and up to 4 hours before serving.

2. Serve the shrimp on a platter with the sauce on the side for dipping.

Sherry Vinegar–Marinated Shrimp Wrapped in Serrano Ham with Piquillo Dipping Sauce

I think this might just incorporate all of my favorite Spanish ingredients into one tasty bite. Sherry vinegar is slightly sweet yet still sharp and I love to use it in marinades as well as vinaigrettes. It's definitely something worth adding to your pantry. While I have noted possible substitutions for both piquillo peppers and Serrano ham in the recipe, if possible, try looking for the real deals for a truly authentic taste of Spain.

Serves 4

3 tablespoons aged sherry vinegar
1 teaspoon Dijon mustard
3 cloves garlic, finely chopped
¼ cup olive oil
1 tablespoon finely chopped fresh thyme leaves

1 pound extra-jumbo (16 to 20 count) shrimp, shelled and deveined
Kosher salt and freshly ground black pepper
12 paper-thin slices Serrano ham or prosciutto, sliced in half lengthwise
Piquillo Dipping Sauce (recipe follows)

224

1. Whisk together the vinegar, mustard, garlic, olive oil, and thyme in a large bowl. Add the shrimp and toss to coat in the mixture. Cover and refrigerate for 30 minutes.

2. Heat your grill to high.

3. Remove the shrimp from the marinade and season with salt and pepper. Place the shrimp on the grates of the grill in an even layer and grill until golden brown and slightly charred, 1½ to 2 minutes. Turn the shrimp over and continue grilling until just cooked through, 45 seconds to 1 minute longer.

4. Remove the shrimp to a platter and wrap each shrimp with a half slice of the ham. Serve with the piquillo dipping sauce.

Piquillo Dipping Sauce

Makes 1½ cups

1¼ cups mayonnaise

1 tablespoon aged sherry vinegar

4 cloves garlic, chopped

4 piquillo peppers or 1 large jarred roasted red
   bell pepper, seeded and chopped

2 teaspoons finely chopped fresh thyme leaves

Kosher salt and freshly ground black pepper

3 tablespoons finely chopped fresh flat-leaf
   parsley leaves

Combine the mayonnaise, vinegar, 2 tablespoons water, garlic, piquillo peppers, and thyme in a blender or food processor and process until smooth. Season with salt and black pepper. Scrape the sauce into a bowl and stir in the parsley. Cover and refrigerate for at least 15 minutes before serving. The sauce can be made 1 day in advance and refrigerated. Do not add the parsley until ready to serve.

Pickled Grilled Shrimp

Pickled shrimp are normally cooked in a seasoned brine and then stored in the refrigerator for several days before serving. I found that grilling the shrimp first as opposed to boiling them adds a touch of smokiness and added texture to this delicious, southern-inspired preparation. You can serve these addictive tangy shrimp as a main course, in smaller portions as an appetizer, or atop a fresh green salad.

Serves 4

¾ cup apple cider vinegar

2 teaspoons kosher salt

2 teaspoons sugar

1 teaspoon coriander seeds

1 teaspoon mustard seeds

1 teaspoon whole black peppercorns

¼ teaspoon red chile flakes

1 cup extra-virgin olive oil

1 medium red onion, halved and thinly
   sliced

4 cloves garlic, smashed

1 bay leaf

Perfectly Grilled Shrimp (page 219)

3 tablespoons finely chopped fresh dill

Combine the vinegar, salt, sugar, coriander seeds, mustard seeds, black peppercorns, and chile flakes in a large bowl. Slowly whisk in the olive oil. Stir in the onion, garlic, bay leaf, and grilled shrimp and toss to coat with the mixture. Cover and refrigerate, stirring every 2 hours, for at least 8 hours, or up to 24 hours. Stir in the fresh dill just before serving. Serve chilled.

Grilled Spice-Rubbed Shrimp "Niçoise" Salad

I think I've made my love of the Niçoise salad pretty clear by this point. And while the original is fantastic, I think the components of this fresh and beautiful French salad are really fun to play around with by creating new arrangements and adding new star ingredients. Here, I substitute spice-rubbed shrimp for the traditional tuna. Instead of laying out anchovy fillets as a part of the salad itself, I incorporate their rich salinity into the vinaigrette for a super-flavorful dressing. Grilling the potatoes gives extra visual appeal and extra flavor. Put it all together—the golden grilled potatoes, fresh yellow and green beans, slivers of purple onion, rosy shrimp, green herbs—and it's a thing of beauty.

Serves 4

Salad
Kosher salt
4 ounces fresh wax beans
4 ounces fresh green beans
1 pound fingerling potatoes
2 tablespoons olive oil
Freshly ground black pepper
½ pound red and yellow grape or cherry tomatoes, halved
1 medium red onion, thinly sliced
2 tablespoons coarsely chopped fresh basil leaves
2 tablespoons coarsely chopped fresh flat-leaf parsley leaves
Niçoise Vinaigrette (recipe follows)

Spice-Rubbed Shrimp
4 teaspoons ground fennel seed
1½ teaspoons dry mustard
1½ teaspoons ground coriander
2 teaspoons kosher salt
½ teaspoon freshly ground black pepper
1 pound jumbo (21 to 25 count) shrimp, shelled and deveined
¼ cup olive oil

1. Fill a large bowl halfway with ice water and set aside.

2. Bring a medium pot of salted cold water to a boil. Add the yellow and green beans and cook for 3 to 4 minutes, or until just crisp-tender. Drain and immediately plunge into the ice water to stop the cooking. Let sit in the ice water for a few minutes, and then drain well.

3. Meanwhile, put the potatoes in a medium saucepan, cover with salted cold water, and bring to a boil. Lower the heat and simmer until the potatoes are almost cooked through (a knife or skewer inserted into the center should meet just a little resistance), 8 to 10 minutes. Drain well and let cool slightly.

(continued)

4. Heat your grill to high.

5. Once cool enough to handle, slice the potatoes lengthwise, brush with 2 table-spoons of the olive oil, and season with salt and pepper. Place on the grill, cut side down, and cook until golden brown, 2 to 3 minutes. Turn over and grill until just cooked through, 1 to 2 minutes longer. Keep the grill on.

6. Combine the cooked beans, grilled potatoes, tomatoes, onion, basil, and parsley in a large bowl. Add the vinaigrette and gently toss to combine. Season with salt and pepper. Cover and let sit at room temperature while you prepare the shrimp.

7. To make the spice rub, combine the fennel, mustard, and coriander with the salt and pepper in a bowl.

8. Put the shrimp in a large bowl and toss with the spice rub until evenly coated. Add the ¼ cup olive oil and toss to coat. Place the shrimp on the grates of the grill in an even layer and grill until golden brown and slightly charred, 1½ to 2 minutes. Turn the shrimp over and continue grilling until just cooked through, 45 seconds to 1 minute longer.

9. Arrange the salad on 4 large plates and top with the shrimp.

Niçoise Vinaigrette

Makes ¾ cup

¼ cup white wine vinegar
2 teaspoons Dijon mustard
1 teaspoon honey
1 clove garlic, finely chopped

1 tablespoon anchovy paste
Kosher salt and freshly ground black pepper
½ cup extra-virgin olive oil

Whisk together the vinegar, mustard, honey, garlic, and anchovy paste and season with salt and pepper. Slowly whisk in the olive oil.

Grilled Shrimp with Tomatillo-Horseradish Sauce

This has quickly become a Bar Americain favorite. The restaurant is an outlet for me to present my takes on classic American dishes, and there is no doubt that shrimp with cocktail sauce belongs in that category. I've kept one aspect of traditional cocktail sauce—horseradish—but the rest is totally original, and absolutely delicious. Tomatillos are one of my favorite southwestern ingredients, and I love how their tart and citrusy taste is pumped up with garlic and jalapeños. I puree spinach into the sauce, which, in addition to adding body, really kicks up the green color of the tomatillos. It's a truly vibrant sauce, both in taste and in appearance.

Serves 4

10 tomatillos, husked and rinsed
1 medium red onion, cut into ½-inch-thick slices
2 jalapeño chiles
2 tablespoons canola oil
Kosher salt and freshly ground black pepper
4 cloves roasted garlic (see page 38)
3 tablespoons rice wine vinegar

¼ cup prepared horseradish, drained
¼ cup chopped fresh cilantro leaves
¼ cup frozen chopped spinach, thawed and squeezed dry
1 tablespoon honey
Perfectly Grilled Shrimp (page 219)

1. Heat your grill to high.

2. Brush the tomatillos, onion, and jalapeños with the oil and season with salt and pepper. Place them on the grates of the grill in an even layer. Grill the tomatillos on all sides until slightly charred and just cooked through, 10 to 12 minutes. Grill the onion slices and jalapeños until slightly charred and just cooked through, 6 to 10 minutes.

3. Transfer the tomatillos, onion slices, and jalapeños to a food processor, add the garlic, and process until smooth. Add the vinegar, horseradish, cilantro, spinach, and honey and pulse 3 to 4 times until just combined. Season with salt and pepper.

4. Serve the shrimp on a platter with the sauce in a small bowl in the center.

squash and eggplant

Grilled Summer Squash and Tomato on Grilled Bread with Ricotta Salata • Grilled Eggplant and Fig Caponata • Grilled Zucchini with Fresh Dill Vinaigrette • Grilled Eggplant and Chickpea Salad • Grilled Eggplant and Manchego Cheese Salad with Balsamic–Black Pepper Glaze • Grilled Eggplant with Fresh Ricotta and Grilled Tomato Relish • Grilled Eggplant Dip with Tomato, Yogurt, and Grilled Bread • Spicy Hoisin-Glazed Eggplant • Orange-Glazed Grilled Acorn Squash

Zucchini and summer squash are classics on the grill. It makes sense; everybody loves to grill in the summer, the same time when gardens across America seemingly shoot out acres of zucchini. But there are more reasons to take zucchini and summer squash to the grill than simple abundance. Their delicate flavor and pale interior really come alive when lit with the grill's smoky taste and crisscrossed with deep brown grill marks. Their texture is also improved by the direct heat of the grill. Zucchini and summer squash are inherently watery vegetables and sometimes become mushy when cooked. Without any pre-salting or draining, grilled zucchini and summer squash stay firm as any excess water quickly evaporates during grilling.

Zucchini and summer squash can be used interchangeably in nearly all preparations. I often like to use a combination of the two for variance in color. Regardless, go with whichever looks best on the shelves when shopping. I prefer them on the small to medium side. I think that they are more flavorful and they are less seedy and watery. Zucchini especially have very fine, delicate skin that is easily bruised and scratched. A small amount of this is fine; just make sure the skin on the whole is smooth and without pits and that the squash is firm, not spongy.

While eggplant technically is a member of the nightshade family, I have always lumped it in with zucchini and summer squash. They look somewhat alike and—especially when it comes to grilling—the methods for preparing them are quite similar. Grilled eggplant is great for a number of reasons. For starters, there's taste: eggplant takes on the rich smokiness of the grill amazingly well. But the grill is tops for eggplant in my book because you can avoid all of those old pitfalls that can leave eggplant soggy and spongy. You don't need to use much oil, which eggplant is notorious for absorbing in copious amounts, and there's no need to salt it and let it sit, because the direct heat of the grill forces out any extra liquid on its own. I seldom prepare eggplant any other way.

When selecting eggplant, I look for ones that are small to medium in size. Bitterness and sponginess tend to occur in the large, overgrown specimens. For this reason I also seek out the small Japanese eggplants for some recipes. The eggplant should be purple all the way up to the stem without any green. It should feel solid in your hand. Fresh eggplant skin is shiny and firm; wrinkled soft skin is a sign of age.

Grilled Summer Squash and Tomato on Grilled Bread with Ricotta Salata

Bread salad is an Italian peasant dish created to make use of stale bread and overly ripe tomatoes. I add another component that there always seems to be too much of at the end of summer, and that's zucchini. Red bell pepper and onion add some sweetness and crunch and ricotta salata adds a nice salty note. If you can't find ricotta salata, feta cheese will work nicely in its place.

Serves 4

1 medium zucchini, halved lengthwise
1 medium yellow squash, halved lengthwise
3 plum tomatoes
1 large red bell pepper
5 tablespoons olive oil
Kosher salt and freshly ground black pepper
1 small red onion, halved and thinly sliced
3 tablespoons red wine vinegar

1 tablespoon fresh lemon juice
2 teaspoons honey
5 cloves garlic, 3 finely chopped, 2 left whole
½ cup extra-virgin olive oil
3 tablespoons finely chopped fresh basil leaves
8 (1-inch-thick) slices French bread or ciabatta, preferably day-old
4 ounces ricotta salata, thinly sliced

1. Heat your grill to high.

2. Brush the zucchini, squash, tomatoes, and bell pepper with the olive oil and season with salt and pepper. Grill the zucchini and squash, cut side down, for 3 to 4 minutes or until lightly golden brown and slightly charred. Turn over and continue grilling until just cooked through, about 4 minutes longer. Grill the tomatoes and bell pepper until charred on all sides, 8 to 10 minutes.

3. Remove the vegetables from the grill, put the bell pepper in a bowl, and cover. Let sit for 10 minutes. Cut the zucchini and squash crosswise into 1-inch pieces. Cut the tomatoes in half lengthwise and coarsely chop. Peel, seed, and finely dice the bell pepper. Combine the zucchini, squash, tomatoes, bell pepper, and onion in a medium bowl.

4. Whisk together the vinegar, lemon juice, honey, and chopped garlic in a small bowl and season with salt and pepper. Slowly whisk in the extra-virgin olive oil until emulsified. Pour the vinaigrette over the vegetables, add the basil, and mix gently to combine. The vegetables can be covered and refrigerated for up to 8 hours. Bring to room temperature before serving.

5. Grill the bread until lightly golden brown on both sides, about 1 minute total. Remove the bread and rub each slice on both sides with the whole garlic cloves.

6. Place the bread on a platter and spoon some of the vegetable mixture and juices over each piece. Top each slice with some of the ricotta salata.

Grilled Eggplant and Fig Caponata

Caponata comes from Sicily and is classically prepared with fried eggplant that is tossed in a sweet-and-sour sauce made with vinegar and sugar. I grill the eggplant, which gives it a sweet and smoky flavor and allows the true flavor of the eggplant to come through. Fresh figs are not normally used in caponata, but I love the additional sweetness they add to the dish. This is a great topping for grilled bread or side dish for grilled chicken or seafood.

Serves 4

1 medium eggplant, cut into ½-inch-thick slices

1 large red onion, peeled and cut into ½-inch-thick slices

3 plum tomatoes, halved

¼ cup olive oil

Kosher salt and freshly ground black pepper

3 cloves garlic, finely chopped

Pinch of red chile flakes

¼ cup red wine vinegar

1 tablespoon honey

½ cup extra-virgin olive oil

6 fresh figs, diced

¼ cup green olives, pitted and chopped

2 tablespoons capers, drained

3 tablespoons golden raisins, plumped in hot water and drained

2 tablespoons pine nuts, toasted (see page 19)

3 tablespoons finely chopped flat-leaf parsley leaves

1 tablespoon finely chopped fresh oregano leaves

1. Heat your grill to high.

2. Brush the eggplant, onion slices, and tomatoes with the olive oil and season with salt and pepper to taste. Grill the eggplant for 6 to 8 minutes per side until golden brown and cooked through. Grill the onions for 3 to 4 minutes per side until golden brown and just cooked through. Grill the tomatoes for 2 minutes per side until charred and slightly soft. Remove the vegetables from the grill and cut into ½-inch dice.

3. Whisk together the garlic, chile flakes, vinegar, honey, and extra-virgin olive oil in a large bowl and season with salt and pepper. Add the eggplant, onion, tomatoes, figs, olives, capers, raisins, pine nuts, parsley, and oregano and mix until combined. Let the mixture sit at room temperature for at least 30 minutes before serving or cover and refrigerate for up to 1 day. Bring to room temperature before serving.

Grilled Zucchini with Fresh Dill Vinaigrette

Chances are you've encountered one of those fancy baskets for grilling vegetables. Personally, I have no use for them. If you're worried about your vegetables falling through the grates of the grill, just cut them bigger or grill them whole! Here, I cut the zucchini into quarters for grilling and then cut them smaller after they have cooked. It works for me! It's vital that you dress the zucchini with the vinaigrette while they are still hot so that all that bright, dilly flavor can seep deep into the flesh of the zucchini.

Serves 4

3 tablespoons white wine vinegar
1 tablespoon fresh lemon juice
2 teaspoons honey
2 teaspoons Dijon mustard

4 tablespoons chopped fresh dill
Kosher salt and freshly ground black pepper
½ cup plus 3 tablespoons olive oil
3 medium zucchini, quartered lengthwise

1. Heat your grill to high.

2. Combine the vinegar, lemon juice, honey, mustard, 3 tablespoons of the dill, and salt and pepper to taste in a blender and blend until smooth. With the motor running, slowly add ½ cup of the oil and blend until emulsified.

3. Brush the zucchini with the remaining 3 tablespoons oil and season with salt and pepper. Grill until lightly golden brown on all sides and just cooked through, about 8 minutes.

4. Remove from the grill and cut each quarter in half crosswise. Place on a platter and immediately drizzle with the vinaigrette. Garnish with the remaining tablespoon dill.

Grilled Eggplant and Chickpea Salad

Eggplant and chickpeas are used together all the time in Middle Eastern cooking, either in the same dish such as here, or paired as components of a meze platter. There is a lot of crossover in Mediterranean and Middle Eastern cuisines, and I have made the most of that here with the additions of grilled peppers, Greek Kalamata olives, mint, and cilantro. And, while the salad is good enough on its own, you could add some crumbled feta to the mix to really put it over the top. This salad is one to try to make in advance (or hope for leftovers), as it gets better and better the longer it sits in the refrigerator.

Serves 4

3 medium Japanese eggplants, halved lengthwise
1 large red bell pepper
1 large yellow bell pepper
6 tablespoons canola oil
Kosher salt and freshly ground black pepper
1 (15.5-ounce) can chickpeas, drained, rinsed, and drained again
1 small red onion, halved and thinly sliced

½ cup Kalamata olives, pitted and coarsely chopped
Juice of 1 lemon
¼ cup extra-virgin olive oil
¼ teaspoon red chile flakes
2 tablespoons finely chopped fresh mint leaves
2 tablespoons finely chopped fresh cilantro leaves

1. Heat your grill to high.

2. Brush the eggplants and bell peppers with the canola oil on all sides and season with salt and pepper. Grill the eggplants for 3 to 4 minutes per side or until lightly golden brown and slightly charred. Grill the bell peppers until charred on all sides and soft, 8 to 10 minutes. Remove the eggplant from the grill and cut each half crosswise into ½-inch-thick slices. Put the peppers in a bowl, wrap and let sit for 10 minutes. Peel, seed, and thinly slice both peppers.

3. Combine the eggplant, red and yellow peppers, chickpeas, onion, and olives in a large bowl. Add the lemon juice, olive oil, chile flakes, mint, and cilantro and stir to combine. Cover and let sit at room temperature for 30 minutes before serving or refrigerate for at least 8 hours and up to 2 days before serving. Serve cold or at room temperature.

Grilled Eggplant and Manchego Cheese Salad with Balsamic–Black Pepper Glaze

This recipe was on the menu of my restaurant Bolo for many years and was always a best seller. I baked it at the restaurant, but when making it for friends and family at home I like to prepare it on the grill; it's a hit either way, but the grilled version is lighter and slightly easier. This makes an excellent vegetarian entrée with its creamy cheese, rich balsamic glaze, and meaty-tasting and -textured eggplant, but it could also be served as a salad course to start off any meal. See photograph on page 230.

Serves 4

2 cups balsamic vinegar
2 teaspoons honey
¼ teaspoon coarsely ground black pepper
3 medium eggplants, cut crosswise into ¼-inch-thick slices (you will need 12 equal slices)

⅓ cup olive oil
Kosher salt and freshly ground black pepper
8 (¼-inch-thick) slices manchego cheese
16 fresh basil leaves, plus 2 tablespoons chopped fresh basil leaves

1. Pour the balsamic vinegar into a medium saucepan and boil over high heat until reduced to ½ cup, about 10 to 12 minutes. Stir in the honey and coarsely ground black pepper and transfer to a bowl. The glaze can be made 1 day in advance, covered, and refrigerated. Bring to room temperature before using.

2. Heat your grill to high.

3. Brush both sides of the eggplant with the oil and season with salt and pepper. Place the eggplant on the grill and grill until golden brown and slightly charred, about 4 minutes. Turn over and continue grilling until just cooked through, 4 to 5 minutes longer. Keep the grill on.

4. Transfer 8 slices of the eggplant to a flat surface, top each slice with a slice of cheese and 2 basil leaves, and season with salt and pepper. Stack the eggplant slices to make four 2-layer stacks and top with the remaining 4 eggplant slices.

5. Carefully return the stacks to the grill and grill for 2 minutes, or until the cheese is slightly melted. Remove the stacks to a large dinner plate, drizzle with the balsamic–black pepper glaze, and garnish with chopped basil.

Grilled Eggplant with Fresh Ricotta and Grilled Tomato Relish

Eggplant Rollatini can be found in just about every southern Italian restaurant in America and with good reason. What's not to love about creamy ricotta wrapped inside eggplant that's baked in the oven with lots of garlicky tomato sauce? My version is lighter, quicker, and every bit as satisfying. Sheep's-milk ricotta is sweet and tangy and if you can find it, you should definitely use it. If it's not available where you live, by all means use the cow's-milk ricotta in the refrigerated section of your grocery store.

Serves 4

2 medium eggplants, cut into ½-inch-thick slices
¼ cup olive oil
Kosher salt and freshly ground black pepper
16 ounces fresh sheep's-milk ricotta

¼ cup finely chopped fresh flat-leaf parsley leaves
1 (2-ounce) block Parmigiano-Reggiano, thinly shaved
Grilled Tomato Relish (page 210)

1. Heat your grill to high.

2. Brush the eggplant slices on both sides with the olive oil and season with salt and pepper. Grill the eggplant until golden brown and cooked through, 4 to 5 minutes per side.

3. Stir together the ricotta and parsley in a medium bowl and season with salt and pepper.

4. Place the grilled eggplant on a large platter and top each slice with a heaping tablespoon of the ricotta mixture, a heaping tablespoon of the tomato relish, and a few shavings of Parmigiano-Reggiano.

Grilled Eggplant Dip with Tomato, Yogurt, and Grilled Bread

This is my version of a Greek dip called *melitzanosalata*. Grilling the eggplants whole gives the sweet flesh an amazing smoky flavor while the yogurt, vinegar, and lemon juice add a fresh tang. I like this served on pieces of good crusty bread for a kind of Greek bruschetta, but it works equally as well as a dip with homemade or store-bought baked pita chips.

Serves 4 to 6

2 medium eggplants
4 tablespoons canola oil
3 plum tomatoes
Kosher salt and freshly ground black pepper
2 cloves garlic
1 small red onion, coarsely chopped
¼ cup Greek yogurt
2 tablespoons red wine vinegar

2 tablespoons fresh lemon juice
1 tablespoon honey
½ cup extra-virgin olive oil
2 tablespoons chopped fresh oregano leaves
¼ cup plus 2 tablespoons chopped fresh flat-leaf parsley leaves
1 long French baguette, cut into 12 slices

240

1. Heat your grill to high.

2. Prick the entire surface of each eggplant with a fork, brush with 3 tablespoons of the canola oil, and place on the grill. Brush the tomatoes with the remaining tablespoon canola oil. Season the tomatoes with salt and pepper and place on the grill. Grill the eggplants, turning occasionally, until soft and their skins are blackened, about 15 minutes. Grill the tomatoes, turning occasionally, until soft and their skins are blackened, about 8 minutes. Remove the eggplants and tomatoes from the grill and let cool slightly. Keep the grill on.

3. Slice the eggplant in half and scoop out the flesh. Place the flesh in the bowl of a food processor. Add the tomatoes, garlic, onion, yogurt, vinegar, lemon juice, honey, ¼ cup of the olive oil, the oregano, and ¼ cup of the parsley and process until smooth. Scrape into a bowl and garnish with the remaining 2 tablespoons chopped parsley.

4. Brush the bread on both sides with the remaining ¼ cup olive oil and season with salt and pepper. Grill for 20 to 30 seconds per side until golden brown and slightly charred.

5. Serve the bread on a platter with the dip in a bowl in the center.

Spicy Hoisin-Glazed Eggplant

Sometimes referred to as Chinese barbecue sauce, hoisin sauce is a nice match with eggplant, one of Asian cuisines' favorite vegetables. Hoisin sauce, which is made from soybean paste, garlic, chiles, sugar, and vinegar, has this great balance between salty and sweet that I really like, and its thick consistency and deep color make for a beautiful glaze. I punch up the already present spiciness of the hoisin sauce with the addition of fresh ginger, garlic, and red chile flakes. Sliced green onions are more than a pretty garnish; they add a subtle yet important layer of crunchy texture and fresh flavor.

Serves 4

5 tablespoons canola oil
1 (1-inch) piece fresh ginger, peeled and grated
2 cloves garlic, finely chopped
1 teaspoon red chile flakes
½ cup hoisin sauce
1 tablespoon rice wine vinegar

1 tablespoon low-sodium soy sauce
2 medium eggplants, cut into ½-inch-thick slices
Kosher salt and freshly ground black pepper
2 green onions, white and green parts, thinly sliced

1. Heat 1 tablespoon of the oil in a small saucepan over medium heat. Add the ginger, garlic, and chile flakes and cook until soft, 3 to 4 minutes. Remove from the heat and whisk in the hoisin, vinegar, and soy sauce until combined.

2. Heat your grill to high.

3. Brush the eggplant slices on both sides with the remaining 4 tablespoons oil and season with salt and pepper. Place the slices on the grill and grill until golden brown and slighty charred, 4 to 5 minutes. Brush with some of the glaze, turn over, and continue grilling just until cooked through, brushing with more of the glaze, 3 to 4 minutes longer.

4. Remove from the grill and brush with the remaining glaze. Transfer to a platter and sprinkle with the green onions.

Orange-Glazed Grilled Acorn Squash

Acorn squash are really beautiful, with orange flesh and a ridged, deep green exterior, and I like to showcase that by serving them halved, not cut up or mashed. Acorn squash, like other winter squashes such as butternut, are naturally sweet and I like preparing them with flavors that enhance that sweetness. This orange glaze does just that. In addition, its sugars caramelize with the heat of the grill, which not only makes the squash taste great, but makes them look gorgeous as well.

Serves 4 to 8

Grated zest of 1 orange
4 cups orange juice (not from concentrate)
½ cup light brown sugar
6 whole allspice berries
2 cinnamon sticks

2 tablespoons unsalted butter, cold
4 acorn squash, halved lengthwise, seeds and membranes removed
Kosher salt and freshly ground black pepper

1. Heat your grill to medium.

2. While the squash is cooking, combine the orange zest, orange juice, brown sugar, allspice, and cinnamon in a medium saucepan and boil over high heat, stirring often until reduced to 1 cup, about 15 minutes. Remove from the heat. Discard the allspice and cinnamon and whisk the butter into the glaze.

3. Meanwhile, put the squash in a large microwave-safe bowl, add ¼ cup water, and cover the bowl with plastic wrap. Poke a few holes in the plastic wrap and microwave on high for 10 minutes.

4. Brush the cut sides of the acorn squash with some of the glaze and season with salt and pepper. Place cut side down on the grill, close the cover, and grill until golden brown, 5 to 7 minutes. Turn the squash over, close the lid, and continue grilling until the center of each squash goes in with a little resistance, about 20 minutes, brushing with the remaining glaze every two minutes.

5. Remove the squash from the grill and brush with any remaining glaze.

tuna

Perfectly Grilled Tuna Steaks • Grilled Tuna with Fennel-Orange Relish, Almonds, and Mint • Grilled Tuna with Grilled Sweet Onion Vinaigrette • Grilled Tuna with Lime-Ginger Butter • Grilled Tuna with Provençal-Style Relish • Three-Chile Glazed Grilled Tuna • Grilled Tuna with Sicilian Sweet-and-Sour Relish • Fennel-Rubbed Tuna Steaks with Saffron–Grilled Red Pepper Sauce and Grilled Oranges • Grilled Tuna Niçoise Sandwich

Growing up, the only tuna I encountered came out of a can. While I have since dis-covered delicious imported oil-packed varieties, I think it's fair to say that the sushi craze opened people up to a whole different tuna experience: the raw kind. But there's a middle step, one between the raw and the preserved, and that's where my love for tuna lies.

Seared on a hot grill, a thick tuna steak will develop a beautiful crust. Cooking it like a steak to rare to medium-rare always gives the best results with a juicy pink interior. Crusty on the outside, juicy inside, grilled tuna is capable of being both delicate, which it is in flavor, and hearty, as its meaty texture makes even the most highly flavored preparations appropriate. I prefer not to take my tuna out of the refrigerator until just before it goes on the grill. I keep it in the fridge both to main-tain its freshness and to help keep the interior cool and stave off overcooking as the exterior is being seared.

Since I do highly recommend that you never cook tuna past medium-rare, it is very important to seek out the freshest cuts. There are several varieties of tuna, among them blackfin, or bigeye; bluefin, which is prized for raw use because of its high fat content; mild yellowfin; and the mildest, least dense kind, albacore. Whichever you choose, make sure that the flesh is firm and glistening, with a fresh, never fishy smell and a clear, bright, deep pink color.

Perfectly Grilled Tuna Steaks

Mild in flavor, meaty in texture, and great as is, a perfectly grilled tuna steak is also a fantastic base for countless tasty combinations of salsas, sauces, and relishes. I look for tuna steaks that are approximately 1 inch thick. Go any thinner than that and the inside will be overcooked by the time the exterior crust develops, and I like my tuna steaks with a cool pink interior and a nice, slightly charred outer crust. Heating your grill to high is a good way to ensure that you'll get that steak-like crust without sacrificing a medium rare temperature.

Serves 4

4 (8-ounce) tuna steaks
2 tablespoons canola or olive oil

Kosher salt and freshly ground black pepper

1. Heat your grill to high.

2. Brush the tuna on both sides with the oil and season with salt and pepper. Place the fillets on the grill and grill until golden brown and slightly charred, 3 to 4 minutes. Flip the fish over and cook to medium-rare, 1 to 2 minutes longer.

Grilled Tuna with Fennel-Orange Relish, Almonds, and Mint

This dish was inspired by a trip to Sicily a few years ago. Fennel, oranges, and mint are a classic combination that is served with many fish dishes. I particularly love this relish with the meaty texture of tuna but it would be lovely with any of the fish in the White Fish chapter (see page 261) as well as with grilled shrimp and even pork and chicken.

Serves 4

1 medium bulb fennel, sliced into ½-inch-thick slices
2 tablespoons canola oil
Kosher salt and freshly ground black pepper
3 oranges
2 tablespoons red wine vinegar

3 tablespoons chopped fresh mint leaves
¼ cup extra-virgin olive oil
¼ cup sliced almonds, toasted (see page 19)
Perfectly Grilled Tuna Steaks (page 247)
Fennel fronds, for garnish, optional

1. Heat your grill to high.

2. Brush the fennel with the canola oil and season with salt and pepper to taste. Grill for 3 to 4 minutes per side or until slightly charred and almost cooked through.

3. While the fennel is cooking, slice off the tops and bottoms of the oranges. Stand each orange on one flat end and slice off the peel and white pith. Working over a bowl to catch the juices, cut between the membranes to release the segments. Squeeze the empty membranes to release any juice.

4. Combine the fennel, orange segments and their juice, red wine vinegar, and mint in a medium bowl, add the olive oil, and season with salt and pepper. The relish can be made 8 hours in advance, covered, and refrigerated. Bring to room temperature and stir in the almonds just before serving.

5. Top the tuna with some of the relish.

Grilled Tuna with Grilled Sweet Onion Vinaigrette

Because tuna is so meat-like, it can stand up to this vinaigrette. I love sweet onions and use them in many of my recipes. If you can't find sweet onions in your market, you can definitely substitute red or yellow onions; just add a little extra honey to the vinegar-oil mixture before adding the onions. This vinaigrette would also pair well with pork, beef, or chicken.

Serves 4

2 sweet onions (such as Vidalia or Walla Walla), sliced into ¼-inch-thick slices
5 tablespoons canola oil
Kosher salt and freshly ground black pepper
¼ cup aged sherry or balsamic vinegar
2 teaspoons honey

⅓ cup extra-virgin olive oil
2 teaspoons finely chopped fresh thyme leaves
2 tablespoons chopped fresh flat-leaf parsley leaves
Perfectly Grilled Tuna Steaks (page 247)

1. Heat your grill to high.

2. Brush the onion slices on both sides with 3 tablespoons of the canola oil and season with salt and pepper. Grill for 3 to 4 minutes per side or until golden brown and just cooked through. Remove from the grill, let cool slightly, and then coarsely chop.

3. Whisk together the vinegar, honey, extra-virgin olive oil, thyme, and parsley in a medium bowl. Add the onions and stir to combine. Let sit at room temperature for at least 15 minutes before serving. The onion vinaigrette can be made 1 day in advance, covered, and refrigerated. Bring to room temperature before serving.

4. Spoon some of the sauce over each tuna steak just as the tuna is removed from the grill.

Grilled Tuna with Lime-Ginger Butter

Think of this lime-ginger butter as *beurre blanc* without the hassle. It has the same ingredients as are found in the classic French butter sauce—shallots, acid, and butter—but prepared quickly in a food processor and not on top of the stove. Once the flavored butter hits the hot tuna, it melts into a smooth, creamy, full-flavored butter sauce. If you have extra limes on hand, grill them (see page 192) and serve alongside for squeezing on top.

Serves 4

1 tablespoon canola oil
1 large shallot, chopped
1 (2-inch) piece fresh ginger, peeled and
 coarsely chopped
Grated zest of 1 lime
1 cup fresh lime juice
1 tablespoon low-sodium soy sauce

2 teaspoons honey
8 tablespoons (1 stick) unsalted butter,
 at room temperature
¼ teaspoon kosher salt
¼ teaspoon freshly ground black pepper
Perfectly Grilled Tuna Steaks (page 247)

1. Heat the oil in a small saucepan over high heat. Add the shallot and ginger and cook until soft, 2 to 3 minutes. Add the lime zest and juice and simmer until the juice is reduced to 2 tablespoons, about 7 minutes. Whisk in the soy sauce and honey, remove from the heat, and let cool for 5 minutes.

2. Combine the shallot mixture, butter, salt, and pepper in a food processor and process until smooth. Scrape the butter into a bowl, cover, and refrigerate until it is chilled and the flavors have melded, about 1 hour. The butter can be made up to 2 days in advance. Remove from the refrigerator 5 minutes before serving.

3. Top the tuna with some of the butter just as the tuna comes off the grill.

Grilled Tuna with Provençal-Style Relish

Don't let the French name of this relish scare you; it's really just a Mediterranean salsa with lots and lots of flavor. Try to make the sauce at least 30 minutes in advance and allow it to sit at room temperature so the flavors can really meld and intensify before serving. You can use this sauce with any fish, and it's just as good with chicken or served on slices of grilled French bread.

Serves 4

3 plum tomatoes, halved, seeded, and finely diced
½ small red onion, finely diced
¼ cup finely chopped Niçoise olives
2 tablespoons capers, drained and finely chopped
2 cloves garlic, finely chopped
3 tablespoons finely chopped fresh basil leaves

3 tablespoons finely chopped fresh mint leaves
Grated zest of 1 lemon
Juice of 1 lemon
¼ cup extra-virgin olive oil
Kosher salt and freshly ground black pepper
Perfectly Grilled Tuna Steaks (page 247)
Fresh basil or mint sprigs, for garnish (optional)

1. Combine the tomatoes, onion, olives, capers, garlic, chopped basil and mint, lemon zest and juice, and olive oil in a medium bowl and season with salt and pepper. Let the sauce sit at room temperature for 30 minutes or refrigerate for up to 2 hours. Bring to room temperature before serving.

2. Spoon the sauce over the hot tuna steaks and garnish with basil sprigs.

Three-Chile Glazed Grilled Tuna

It is hard to believe that such a flavorful glaze could be so easy to prepare, but it's true. I was introduced to habanero powder a few years ago and immediately fell in love with its spicy flavor and floral undertones. Just like fresh habaneros, the powder is assertive; only a small amount of the powder is needed to yield the full impact of the chile. Because tuna has a meat-like taste and texture, it can handle the strong flavor of this glaze; but you could also use it on lamb, chicken, and even beef.

Serves 4

1 cup honey
1 heaping tablespoon Dijon mustard
1 tablespoon ancho chile powder
1 tablespoon New Mexican red chile powder

2 teaspoons habanero chile powder
Kosher salt
4 (8-ounce) tuna steaks
2 tablespoons canola oil

1. Whisk together the honey, mustard, the three chile powders, and ¼ teaspoon salt in a small bowl. Let sit at room temperature for 30 minutes before using to allow the chile powders to bloom.

2. Heat your grill to high.

3. Brush the tuna steaks on both sides with the oil and season with salt. Place the steaks on the grill and grill until golden brown and slightly charred, 3 to 4 minutes. Brush the top side of the tuna liberally with the glaze, flip over, and continue cooking to medium-rare, 1 to 2 minutes longer.

4. Remove from the grill, place glaze side up on a platter, and immediately brush the tuna with more of the glaze.

Grilled Tuna with Sicilian Sweet-and-Sour Relish

Thin slices of tuna quickly grilled and topped with this sweet-and-sour relish from Sicily are perfect for a light summer meal or served over peppery greens like arugula or watercress for a simple lunchtime salad.

Serves 4

1 cup red wine vinegar
3 tablespoons sugar
3 tablespoons raisins
1 red bell pepper, grilled (see page 120), peeled, seeded, and thinly sliced
1 yellow bell pepper, grilled (see page 120), peeled, seeded, and thinly sliced
2 tablespoons capers, drained

2 tablespoons extra-virgin olive oil
2 tablespoons finely chopped fresh flat-leaf parsley leaves, plus whole sprigs for garnish
Kosher salt and freshly ground black pepper
4 (8-ounce) tuna steaks, cut into ¼-inch-thick slices
2 tablespoons olive oil

1. Combine the vinegar, sugar, and raisins in a small saucepan and boil over high heat until the sugar melts and the vinegar reduces by half, about five minutes.

2. Combine the red and yellow peppers and capers in a medium bowl. Add the raisin mixture, extra-virgin olive oil, and the chopped parsley and stir to combine. Season the mixture with salt and pepper and let sit at room temperature for 30 minutes before serving. The relish can be made 1 day in advance and refrigerated. Bring to room temperature before serving.

3. Heat your grill to high.

4. Brush the tuna on both sides with the olive oil and season with salt and pepper. Grill the tuna for 1 to 2 minutes per side.

5. Divide the tuna among 4 plates and immediately spoon some of the relish on top. Garnish with parsley sprigs.

Fennel-Rubbed Tuna Steaks with Saffron–Grilled Red Pepper Sauce and Grilled Oranges

This dish is a perfect example of why I love tuna—it stands its own against the boldest flavorings, such as this savory fennel rub. Assertive and intriguing, saffron is heralded as one of the stand-out seasonings of Spanish cuisine. It's expensive, as a tremendous amount of work goes into producing even a minuscule quantity, but it's worth the splurge as nothing else tastes quite like it. Saffron will also keep for quite some time if properly stored in a cool, dark place. The red peppers in the sauce only intensify the vibrant orange-red color lent by the saffron. As a final touch, grilled oranges provide a sweet hit of juice as well as a beautiful garnish.

Serves 4

1½ tablespoons ground fennel seeds
2 teaspoons kosher salt
½ teaspoon freshly ground black pepper
4 (8-ounce) tuna steaks
3 tablespoons olive oil

2 oranges, halved crosswise
Saffron–Grilled Red Pepper Sauce (recipe follows)
2 tablespoons finely chopped fresh chives

256

1. Heat your grill to high.

2. Combine the fennel, salt, and pepper in a small bowl. Brush both sides of the tuna steaks with 2 tablespoons of the oil and season both sides with the spice mixture.

3. Place the steaks on the grill and grill until golden brown and slightly charred, 3 to 4 minutes. Flip the fish over and cook to medium-rare, 1 to 2 minutes longer.

4. Brush the cut sides of the oranges with the remaining 1 tablespoon oil. Place on the grill, cut side down, and grill until slightly charred and just warmed through, 2 to 3 minutes.

5. Spoon or drizzle some of the sauce onto 4 large plates and top each with a tuna steak. Squeeze the juice of the grilled oranges over the tuna and sprinkle with the chives.

Saffron–Grilled Red Pepper Sauce

Makes approximately 1 cup

8 tablespoons olive oil
1 small Spanish onion, finely chopped
2 cloves garlic, finely chopped
2 large red bell peppers, grilled (see page 120), peeled, seeded, and chopped

Large pinch of saffron
3 tablespoons sherry vinegar
2 teaspoons honey
Kosher salt and freshly ground black pepper

1. Heat 2 tablespoons of the oil in a medium sauté pan over medium heat. Add the onion and garlic and cook until soft, about 5 minutes. Add the red peppers, ½ cup water, and the saffron and bring to a simmer. Cook until the peppers are very soft and the liquid has reduced slightly, 8 to 10 minutes.

2. Transfer the mixture to a blender, add the vinegar, honey, and remaining 6 tablespoons oil and blend until smooth. Season with salt and pepper to taste. If the mixture is too thick to pour, thin it out with a little water. The sauce can be kept refrigerated, covered, for up to 2 days. Bring to room temperature before serving.

Grilled Tuna Niçoise Sandwich

The classic version of this sandwich, which originated in Nice, France, is made with canned tuna, which is delicious, but I love the taste of fresh tuna that has been slightly charred and flaked with a fork. There are a couple of rules to follow when making the sandwich: use a good crusty roll that will hold up to the oil in the dressing, because the longer you let this sandwich sit, the more the flavors soak into the bread, and the better the result. And while I normally cook my tuna to medium-rare, for this recipe, you definitely need to cook it all the way through so that it will flake properly. Don't worry about the tuna being dry; the other ingredients will lend it flavor and moisture.

Serves 2 to 4

3 (8-ounce) tuna steaks
2 tablespoons olive oil
Kosher salt and freshly ground black pepper
1 small red onion, halved and thinly sliced
¾ cup grape or cherry tomatoes, halved
1 tablespoon anchovy paste
2 garlic cloves, finely chopped
2 tablespoons mayonnaise

1 tablespoon grated lemon zest
3 tablespoons fresh lemon juice
2 tablespoons honey
Pinch of cayenne pepper
½ cup extra-virgin olive oil
2 tablespoons capers, drained
3 tablespoons chopped fresh basil leaves
1 French baguette

1. Heat your grill to high.

2. Brush the tuna steaks on both sides with the 2 tablespoons olive oil and season with salt and pepper. Grill for 3 to 4 minutes on both sides until just cooked through. Let rest for 5 minutes and then flake with a fork. Place in a bowl with the red onion and tomatoes. Keep the grill on.

3. Whisk together the anchovy paste, garlic, mayonnaise, lemon zest, lemon juice, honey, cayenne, and the ½ cup extra-virgin olive oil in a small bowl and season with salt. Pour the mixture over the tuna, add the capers and basil, and gently mix to combine.

4. Place the baguette on the grill, close the cover, and let the bread heat through, 3 to 4 minutes. Remove from the grill and slice through lengthwise. Remove some of the inside of the bread. Spread the tuna mixture evenly over the bottom half of the bread, place the top on, and press down firmly on the sandwich. Wrap the sandwich in foil and place a heavy pan on top. Let sit for at least 30 minutes in the refrigerator and up to 1 day before serving. Cut into 4 pieces before serving.

white fish

Jerk-Rubbed Red Snapper with Green Onion and Cilantro • Grilled Halibut with Grilled Pineapple-Jicama Salsa • Grilled Fish Tacos with Chipotle Crema and Salsa Fresca • Grilled Sea Bass with Salsa Verde • Herb-Marinated Grilled Sea Bass with Piquillo Pesto • Honey-Citrus Glazed Cod with Grapefruit-Orange Relish • Grilled Cod with White Bean Relish and Tomato Vinaigrette • Grilled Tilapia with Lemon Butter and Capers

For the purposes of this book, I found it much easier and more user-friendly to create one category entitled "White Fish" than to do separate chapters for red snapper, halibut, striped bass, sea bass, cod, and tilapia. While cooking times may differ slightly and there are subtle differences in taste and texture, all these fish are similar enough to be interchangeable in these recipes. So grab the best flaky white fish that you can find and pick a recipe.

White fish have lean, flaky, and—you've got it—white flesh. As opposed to meatier, darker-fleshed fish such as tuna and salmon, white fish store their fat in their livers, not their muscles, so their sweet and delicate meat is very low in fat.

Due to their lean and light nature, white fish cook quite quickly and can become dry if overcooked. Many people are afraid of grilling fish because they have had bad experiences with fish sticking to the grates of the grill. The best way to avoid this is pretty simple: don't play with your food! Do not move your fish on the grill until it is cooked enough to release on its own.

When purchasing white fish, look for sweet-smelling, firm flesh. It should smell slightly of the sea, not "fishy." If you are buying the whole fish, as you might be with a red snapper or bass, check out the eyes. They should be clear and not at all cloudy. Most of the preparations in this chapter can be made with any white fish. It's always a good idea to design your meal around whichever fish looks the freshest at your fish counter on shopping day; everything else is adaptable.

Jerk-Rubbed Red Snapper with Green Onion and Cilantro

You may be most familiar with jerk-rubbed chicken, but the Caribbean spice mixture, at once spicy, sweet, and savory, works beautifully on red snapper fillets. This is a wet rub; the spices are pulsed to a paste with lime juice and canola oil. This really helps the flavor seep into and adhere to the fish. The finishing touch of minced green onions and cilantro is more than a lovely garnish: the verdant qualities of the two come to life when they hit the warm fish and provide a great spark of freshness to the dish.

Serves 4

1 medium red onion, coarsely chopped
6 green onions, white and green parts, coarsely chopped
2 serrano chiles, coarsely chopped
1 (1-inch) piece fresh ginger, peeled and coarsely chopped
1 clove garlic
1 tablespoon fresh thyme leaves
1 teaspoon ground cinnamon

1 teaspoon ground allspice
½ teaspoon ground cloves
1 teaspoon kosher salt
¼ teaspoon freshly ground black pepper
Juice of 1 lime
¼ cup canola oil
4 (8-ounce) red snapper fillets
¼ cup fresh cilantro leaves

1. Combine the red onion, two-thirds of the green onions, the chiles, ginger, garlic, thyme, cinnamon, allspice, cloves, salt, pepper, lime juice, and canola oil in a food processor and process until the mixture is smooth.

2. Put the snapper in a baking dish and spread a few tablespoons of the mixture over 1 side of each fillet. Let marinate in the refrigerator for 20 minutes.

3. Heat your grill to medium-high.

4. Combine the remaining green onions and the cilantro leaves on a cutting board and chop until very fine.

5. Place the snapper on the grill, rub side down, and cook until golden brown and slightly charred, 3 minutes. Turn the fish over and continue grilling until just cooked through, 3 to 4 minutes longer.

6. Remove the fish from the grill and immediately sprinkle with the green onion–cilantro mixture.

Grilled Halibut with Grilled Pineapple-Jicama Salsa

I love grilled pineapple not only for dessert but also in a relish such as this one served with grilled fish. Jicama tastes like a cross between an apple and a cucumber and has an amazing crunch that complements the soft texture of the grilled pineapple and red bell pepper.

Serves 4

½ small pineapple, peeled, sliced 1 inch thick, and cored
1 red bell pepper
4 tablespoons canola oil
1 small jicama, peeled and finely diced
1 small red onion, finely chopped

2 fresh red chiles (such as Thai bird or Fresno), finely diced
3 tablespoons rice wine vinegar
2 tablespoons extra-virgin olive oil
3 tablespoons finely chopped fresh basil leaves
Kosher salt and freshly ground black pepper
4 (8-ounce) halibut fillets

1. Heat your grill to high.

2. Brush the pineapple and bell pepper with 2 tablespoons of the canola oil. Grill the pineapple until golden brown on both sides, about 6 minutes. Grill the bell pepper until charred on all sides, 8 to 10 minutes. Remove the pineapple from the grill and cut into small dice. Remove the bell pepper from the grill, put it in a bowl, and cover. Let sit for 10 minutes before peeling, seeding, and finely dicing the pepper.

3. Combine the pineapple, bell pepper, jicama, onion, chiles, vinegar, olive oil, and basil in a medium bowl and season with salt and pepper. Let sit at room temperature while you prepare the halibut. The salsa can be made 8 hours in advance, covered, and refrigerated. Bring to room temperature before serving.

4. Brush the halibut on both sides with the remaining 2 tablespoons canola oil and season with salt and pepper. Place the fillets on the grill and cook until golden brown and slightly charred, 3 to 4 minutes. Turn the fish over and continue grilling until just cooked through, 3 to 4 minutes longer.

5. Serve the fish fillets topped with the salsa.

Grilled Fish Tacos with Chipotle Crema and Salsa Fresca

Every time I go to southern California, I search out the nearest taquería and order a few fish tacos, and as I eat them, think I have died and gone to heaven. How can something as humble as a piece of fish folded up in a tortilla with some cabbage and salsa bring so much pleasure? You just need to try them for yourself to figure it out.

Serves 4 to 6

2 pounds flaky white fish fillets (such as red snapper, striped bass, or sea bass)
¼ cup canola oil
1 tablespoon ancho chile powder
2 teaspoons kosher salt
8 (6-inch) white or yellow corn tortillas
Chipotle Crema (recipe follows)

¼ head of white or red cabbage, finely shredded
1 medium white onion, halved and thinly sliced
Fresh cilantro leaves, for serving
Salsa Fresca (recipe follows)
Lime wedges, for serving

1. Heat your grill to high.

2. Brush the fish on both sides with the oil and season with the ancho powder and salt. Place the fillets on the grill and cook until golden brown and slightly charred, 3 to 4 minutes. Turn the fish over and continue grilling until just cooked through, 3 to 4 minutes longer. Remove the fish and let rest for 5 minutes before shredding into bite-sized pieces.

3. While the fish is resting, wrap the tortillas in foil and place on the grill for 5 minutes to warm through.

4. Lay the warm tortillas on a flat surface and drizzle with some of the chipotle crema. Top with fish, cabbage, onion, cilantro leaves, and salsa. Fold and eat with a squeeze of lime juice.

Chipotle Crema

Makes 1 cup

1 cup crème fraîche or sour cream
2 teaspoons pureed canned chipotle chiles in
  adobo

¼ teaspoon kosher salt

Whisk together the crème fraîche, chipotle puree, and salt in a small bowl. Refrigerate for at least 15 minutes or up to 1 day before serving.

Salsa Fresca

Makes 2 cups

3 large ripe beefsteak tomatoes, halved, seeded,
  and finely diced
½ small white onion, finely diced
2 cloves garlic, finely chopped
1 jalapeño or serrano chile, finely diced

Juice of 1 lime
2 tablespoons canola oil
Kosher salt and freshly ground black pepper
3 tablespoons chopped fresh cilantro leaves

Combine the tomatoes, onion, garlic, chile, lime juice, oil, salt, pepper, and cilantro in a medium bowl. Let sit at room temperature for at least 15 minutes before serving. The salsa can be made 2 hours ahead, covered, and refrigerated. Bring to room temperature before serving.

Grilled Sea Bass with Salsa Verde

This full-flavored, fresh green sauce is the Italian version of *salsa verde* and is very different from the southwestern version (made with roasted tomatillos, onions, and lots of cilantro) that you will find at my restaurant Mesa Grill. This vibrant sauce also goes well with grilled chicken, lamb, and beef.

Serves 4

2 cups lightly packed fresh flat-leaf parsley leaves, plus extra whole sprigs for garnish
¼ cup chopped fresh chives
1 tablespoon capers, drained
3 cloves garlic
Juice of 1 lemon
2 anchovy fillets

1 tablespoon Dijon mustard
1 tablespoon honey
½ cup extra-virgin olive oil
4 (8-ounce) sea bass fillets
2 tablespoons canola oil
Kosher salt and freshly ground black pepper
Lemon slices, for garnish (optional)

1. Combine the parsley, chives, capers, garlic, lemon juice, anchovies, mustard, honey, and 2 tablespoons water in a blender or food processor and pulse 5 to 7 times until coarsely chopped. With the motor running, slowly add the extra-virgin olive oil and blend until emulsified. The sauce can be made 4 hours in advance, covered, and refrigerated. Bring to room temperature before serving.

2. Heat your grill to high.

3. Brush the fish on both sides with the canola oil and season with salt and pepper. Grill the fish for 3 to 4 minutes per side or until lightly golden brown and slightly charred.

4. Remove the fish from the grill and top each fillet with some of the salsa verde. Garnish with lemon slices and parsley sprigs, if desired.

Herb-Marinated Grilled Sea Bass with Piquillo Pesto

Fire-roasted and hand-peeled *pimientos del piquillo* (piquillo peppers) are a unique specialty of Navarra, Spain. Unlike red bell peppers, the piquillo is slightly piquant but not hot. They are available online, but if you don't have them on hand, you can substitute grilled red bell peppers in this recipe. I add a little chipotle puree to heighten the spiciness of the pepper, but feel free to leave it out; the pesto will be just as good. This pesto is also great tossed with pasta or mixed into mayonnaise as a condiment for any sandwich or burger.

Serves 4

½ cup fresh flat-leaf parsley leaves, plus more for garnish
¼ cup chopped fresh chives
2 tablespoons fresh thyme leaves
2 cloves garlic, chopped

½ cup olive oil
4 (8-ounce) sea bass fillets
Kosher salt and freshly ground black pepper
Piquillo Pesto (recipe follows)

1. Combine the parsley, chives, thyme, garlic, and olive oil in a blender and blend until smooth. Put the fish fillets in a baking dish, pour the marinade over, and turn to coat. Let marinate for 20 minutes in the refrigerator.

2. Heat your grill to high.

3. Remove the fish from the marinade and season with salt and pepper on both sides. Place the fillets on the grill and cook until golden brown and slightly charred, 3 to 4 minutes. Turn the fish over and continue grilling until just cooked through, 3 to 4 minutes longer.

4. Remove the fillets from the grill, top with some of the piquillo pesto, and garnish with parsley leaves.

Piquillo Pesto

Makes 1 cup

1 (8-ounce) jar piquillo peppers, drained, or
    2 large red bell peppers, grilled (see page
    120), peeled, seeded, and chopped
2 cloves garlic, chopped
3 tablespoons pine nuts
1 tablespoon red wine vinegar
1 teaspoon pureed canned chipotle chiles in
  adobo

½ cup olive oil
5 tablespoons freshly grated Parmigiano-
    Reggiano cheese
1 teaspoon honey
Kosher salt and freshly ground black pepper

Combine the piquillo peppers, garlic, pine nuts, vinegar, and chipotle puree in a food processor and process until coarsely chopped. With the motor running, slowly add the oil and pulse just until combined. Transfer to a bowl and stir in the cheese, honey, and salt and pepper to taste. The pesto can be made 1 day in advance, covered, and refrigerated. Bring to room temperature before serving.

Honey-Citrus Glazed Cod with Grapefruit-Orange Relish

I like to make this dish during those dark, dragging weeks of winter. For one thing, that's when citrus is at the peak of its growing season. But more than that: you bring this plate to the table, and it's just like serving up sunshine. Everything about this cod and relish is bright, fresh, and sunny. This glaze and relish combination is really well balanced: slightly bitter grapefruit and savory red onion keep the relish grounded, and sharply acidic lemon juice and zest counter the super-sweet honey and orange in the glaze.

Serves 4

½ cup orange blossom honey
1 teaspoon grated orange zest
1 teaspoon grated lemon zest
2 tablespoons fresh orange juice
2 tablespoons fresh lemon juice
1½ tablespoons finely chopped fresh oregano
   leaves

Kosher salt
4 (8-ounce) cod fillets
2 tablespoons canola oil
Freshly ground black pepper
Grapefruit-Orange Relish (recipe follows)

1. Whisk together the honey, orange and lemon zest and juice, oregano, and ½ teaspoon salt in a small bowl. Let sit for 15 minutes at room temperature before using.

2. Heat your grill to high.

3. Brush the cod with the oil on both sides and season with salt and pepper. Place the cod on the grill and grill until golden brown and slightly charred, 3 to 4 minutes. Brush the top of the fillets with the honey glaze, turn over, and continue grilling until just cooked through, 3 to 4 minutes longer.

4. Remove the cod from the grill, glaze side up, and brush with more of the glaze.

Grapefruit-Orange Relish

Makes 2 cups

2 fresh oranges, peeled, sectioned (see page 249), and cut into ¼-inch pieces
1 medium grapefruit, peeled, sectioned (see page 249), and cut into ¼-inch pieces
½ small red onion, halved and thinly sliced
Juice of ½ orange

2 tablespoons aged sherry vinegar
2 teaspoons orange blossom honey
1 tablespoon extra-virgin olive oil
3 tablespoons chopped fresh flat-leaf parsley
   leaves
Kosher salt and freshly ground black pepper

Combine the oranges, grapefruit, onion, orange juice, vinegar, honey, oil, and parsley in a medium bowl and season lightly with salt and pepper. Let the relish sit at room temperature for at least 15 minutes before serving. The relish can be made 8 hours in advance, covered, and refrigerated. Bring to room temperature before serving.

Grilled Cod with White Bean Relish and Cherry Tomato Vinaigrette

This dish is a lesson in contrasts, and a perfect example of why that cooking philosophy works so well. White, light, and flaky cod is topped with a rich and creamy bean relish. The warm tomato vinaigrette adds a shot of color and texture—the tomatoes burst from the heat and pop in your mouth. One note: because of its flaky nature, cod can be a bit tricky on the grill. Be sure to oil the fish liberally and use extra care when turning it.

Serves 4

1 pint grape or cherry tomatoes
3 tablespoons olive oil
Kosher salt and freshly ground black pepper
3 tablespoons balsamic vinegar
1 shallot, finely chopped
Pinch of red chile flakes
⅓ cup extra-virgin olive oil

2 tablespoons chopped fresh basil leaves, plus extra sprigs for garnish
2 tablespoons chopped fresh flat-leaf parsley leaves
4 (8-ounce) cod fillets
2 tablespoons canola oil
White Bean Relish (recipe follows)

1. Heat your grill to high.

2. Put the tomatoes in a bowl, toss with the olive oil, and season liberally with salt and pepper. Place the tomatoes on the grill in an even layer and grill until soft and charred on all sides, about 5 minutes for grape tomatoes and 8 minutes for cherry tomatoes.

3. While the tomatoes are grilling, whisk together the vinegar, shallot, and chile flakes in a medium bowl and season with salt and pepper. Slowly whisk in the extra-virgin olive oil until emulsified and then stir in the basil and parsley. Add the hot tomatoes and let sit at room temperature while you prepare the cod.

4. Brush the cod with the canola oil on both sides and season with salt and pepper. Place the cod on the grill and grill until golden brown and slightly charred, 3 to 4 minutes. Turn over and continue grilling until just cooked through, 3 to 4 minutes longer.

5. Remove the cod to a platter and top with the white bean relish and cherry tomato vinaigrette. Garnish with basil sprigs.

White Bean Relish

Makes approximately 3 cups

1 (15.5-ounce) can white beans, drained, rinsed, and drained again
½ cup pitted and chopped Kalamata olives
1 red bell pepper, grilled (see page 120), seeded, and finely diced
1 yellow bell pepper, grilled (see page 120), seeded, and finely diced

½ small red onion, thinly sliced
¼ cup extra-virgin olive oil
2 tablespoons chopped fresh flat-leaf parsley leaves
Kosher salt and freshly ground black pepper

Combine the beans, olives, red and yellow peppers, onion, oil, and parsley in a medium bowl and season with salt and pepper. Let sit at room temperature for at least 30 minutes before serving to allow the flavors to meld. The relish can be made 8 hours in advance and stored, covered, in the refrigerator. Bring to room temperature before serving.

Grilled Tilapia with Lemon Butter and Capers

Tilapia seems to be showing up on menus everywhere today. I have used this flaky white fish for years in my restaurants, but if you can't find it, you can substitute bass or snapper. The butter flavored with lemon and white wine and the sprinkling of the capers at the end is really just a play on piccata, a quick pan sauce normally served over chicken or veal. This recipe is perfect served over rice or orzo, which is a rice-shaped pasta.

Serves 4

Grated zest and juice of 1 lemon
½ cup dry white wine
2 teaspoons honey
8 tablespoons (1 stick) unsalted butter, at room temperature

Kosher salt and freshly ground black pepper
4 (8-ounce) tilapia fillets
2 tablespoons olive oil
¼ cup capers, drained
¼ cup chopped fresh flat-leaf parsley leaves

1. Combine the lemon zest and juice, wine, and honey in a small saucepan over high heat and boil until reduced by half, about 5 minutes. Remove from the heat and let cool. Whisk together the butter and wine mixture in a small bowl and season with salt and pepper. The butter can be made 1 day in advance, covered, and refrigerated. Bring to room temperature before serving.

2. Heat your grill to high.

3. Brush the fish on both sides with the oil and season with salt and pepper. Grill the fish for 3 to 4 minutes per side or until lightly golden brown and slightly charred.

4. Remove the fish from the grill and immediately top each fillet with some of the butter and capers. Garnish with the parsley.

sources

For Spices, Dried Chiles, and Hot Sauces
- www.kalustyans.com, 800-352-3451
- www.penzys.com

For Hot Sauces, Rubs, and Barbecue Sauces
- www.BobbyFlay.com

For Cheeses
- www.dairysection.com

For Fresh Lobsters
- www.mainelobsterdirect.com, 800-556-2783
- www.thelobsternet.com, 800-360-9520

For Fresh Seafood
- www.gortonsfreshseafood.com, 800-335-3674

For Organic Chicken
- www.eberlypoultry.com, 717-336-6440

For Buffalo
- www.buybuffalo.com, 800-543-6328

For Specialty Foods, such as Merguez
- www.gourmetfoodstore.com, 877-591-8008

For Fresh Lobsters, Seafood, Chicken, Duck, and Merguez
- www.citarella.com, 212-874-0383

For Specialty Produce, such as Fresh Chiles
- www.melissas.com, 800-588-0151

For Whole-Grain Products
- www.bobsredmill.com, 800-349-2173

For Spanish Ingredients, such as Piquillo Peppers and Smoked Paprika
- www.tienda.com, 888-472-1022 or 800-710-4304

For Asian Ingredients, such as Miso
- www.asianfoodgrocer.com, 888-482-2742

For Barbecue Wood, Charcoal, Chips, and Planks
- www.barbequewood.com, 800-347-3966
- www.justsmokedsalmon.com, 866-716-2710

For Grilling Accessories
- www.bbqgalore.com, 800-752-3085

For Kitchen Supplies
- www.broadwaypanhandler.com
- www.williams-sonoma.com

For Gas Grills
- www.viking.com

For Charcoal Grills
- www.weber.com

index